Praise

HISTORY MAKERS

Prayer wasn't born in the twenty-first century; it didn't even begin with Jesus! Prayer is found in the Old Testament. As long as people have believed in God, there has been prayer.

Through all these hundreds of years, prayers identical in nature have been offered up to the Lord. Deliverance, salvation and freedom are just a few of the prayers called out through the ages and today.

You will see in *History Makers* that these prayers join in eternity to produce powerful results in God's perfect timing. It is true, we are not alone, we are surrounded by a great cloud of witnesses. Our prayers are mingling in eternity for eternal purposes.

MIKE BICKLE

DIRECTOR, INTERNATIONAL HOUSE OF PRAYER

When I began reading *History Makers*, my spirit was electrified. This book is rich with our nation's history and revival moments. I was a part of the two teams that traveled with Dutch and Will as they took "the kettle" from Jamestown and Williamsburg, Virginia. The presence of God that was so powerful as we visited these historic sites has been captured in Dutch and Will's book. You will feel you are on a journey with our founding fathers to the present day. The synergy of the ages will become an enabling tool to connect us to all past, present and future generations. The holy moves of God throughout *History Makers* are a true part of redigging the wells of revival throughout America. We are joined to the covenants of those who have gone before us. Their voices still speak to us today.

BARBARA BYERLY

DIRECTOR, PRAYER FOR JERICHO CENTER AND EVERY HOME FOR CHRIST
EXECUTIVE BOARD OF NATIONAL PRAYER COMMITTEE AND MISSION
AMERICA FACILITATION COMMITTEE

Walking with God and changing history! What a concept! Our participation in the Kettle Tour with Dutch and Will has however so radically changed our own personal history that now through us the Lord is able to release change into the history of many nations. To understand and accept the invitation put forth by this book of remembrance requires a subtle but history shaping change from the mind of the soul to the mind of the spiritual heart. To more effectively understand its message, place your anointed right hand over your heart and ask the Lord this simple request: "Open the spiritual mind of my heart Lord to hear, see and understand who You are and who I am in You." Here is His promise to you: "If you will allow me to open your heart, then you will see me as I am; that's who you are!" The foundational message of *History Makers* is about godly transformation of nations, which begins and moves forward one liberated person at a time. Its testimonies reestablish and reconnect us to the holy pathway of true living within the context of the spiritual kingdom of God on Earth. In your spiritual heart hear the voice of the Lord calling you to a radical shift from normal Christianity to awaken, rise up and move forward to co-labor with the King of kings and to do His exploits in the power of His kingly anointing as His history makers beginning right where you live.

JIM AND FAITH CHOSA

PASTORS, RED EARTH CHURCH IN THE WILDERNESS
YELLOWTAIL, MONTANA

Dutch Sheets and Will Ford form a powerful writing team. Their model of white and black is by itself a reconciliation statement. It is for all you whose heart desires to heal your nations and bring them back to God. *History Makers* will grip your heart and catapult you into making history rather than talking about it.

CINDY JACOBS

AUTHOR, *THE VOICE OF GOD*
GENERALS OF INTERCESSION

Sincere believers everywhere are asking, How do we fix the mess humankind has made of this world? Dutch Sheets and Will Ford have finally answered the question. Rich in historic data and fresh scriptural insights, this captivating volume should be required reading for people who want to leave a permanent imprint on the sands of time.

HARRY R. JACKSON, JR.
AUTHOR, *HIGH-IMPACT AFRICAN-AMERICAN CHURCHES* AND
IN-LAWS, OUTLAWS AND THE FUNCTIONAL FAMILY

I read the book and I enjoyed it because I enjoy history so much. I enjoyed the history of my people especially during the time of slavery and struggle. Also, I enjoyed the biblical Christian principles that were a part of the book. I really want to endorse this book. I think it is something that all of us should read.

JOHN PERKINS
JOHN PERKINS FOUNDATIONS
COFOUNDER, THE CHRISTIAN COMMUNITY
DEVELOPMENT ASSOCIATION

Prophetic acts, when done under the explicit direction of God, are powerful influences for changing the spiritual atmosphere over a territory. The legendary Kettle Tour was one of the most dramatic sustained prophetic acts in American history. *History Makers* not only tells the fascinating story firsthand, but it also will draw you into the experience, enrich you spiritually and fortify your faith.

C. PETER WAGNER
AUTHOR, *CHANGING CHURCH*
WAGNER LEADERSHIP INSTITUTE

DUTCH SHEETS

HISTORY MAKERS

WILLIAM FORD III

Regal

From Gospel Light
Ventura, California, U.S.A.

PUBLISHED BY REGAL BOOKS
FROM GOSPEL LIGHT
VENTURA, CALIFORNIA, U.S.A.

Regal PRINTED IN THE U.S.A.

Regal Books is a ministry of Gospel Light, a Christian publisher dedicated to serving the local church. We believe God's vision for Gospel Light is to provide church leaders with biblical, user-friendly materials that will help them evangelize, disciple and minister to children, youth and families.

It is our prayer that this Regal book will help you discover biblical truth for your own life and help you meet the needs of others. May God richly bless you.

For a free catalog of resources from Regal Books/Gospel Light, please call your Christian supplier or contact us at 1-800-4-GOSPEL *or* www.regalbooks.com.

All Greek and Hebrew definitions are taken from James Strong, *Strong's Exhaustive Concordance of the Bible* (Peabody, MA: Hendrickson Publishers, 1988).

Cover design by David Griffing
Interior design by Stephen Hahn
Edited by Steven Lawson

Library of Congress Cataloging-in-Publication Data
Sheets, Dutch.
  History makers / Dutch Sheets and William Ford III.
    p. cm.
  Includes index.
  ISBN 0-8307-3245-4
  1. Prayer—Christianity. 2. History—Religious aspects—Christianity. I. Ford, William, 1965- II. Title.
  BV227.S54 2004
  248.3'2—dc22   2004012463

1 2 3 4 5 6 7 8 9 10 11 12 13 14 15 / 10 09 08 07 06 05 04

Rights for publishing this book in other languages are contracted by Gospel Light Worldwide, the international nonprofit ministry of Gospel Light. Gospel Light Worldwide also provides publishing and technical assistance to international publishers dedicated to producing Sunday School and Vacation Bible School curricula and books in the languages of the world. For addi-tional information, visit www.gospellightworld wide.org; write to Gospel Light Worldwide, P.O. Box 3875, Ventura, CA 93006; or send an e-mail to info@gospellightworldwide.org.

DEDICATION

The Sheetses and Fords dedicate this book to You, Jesus. Thank You for being the author and finisher of our history together. We love You!

IN MEMORY

This book is written in memory of a nameless teenaged girl and other unknown heroes of faith in America who saw fit to pass down the memorials and history of God's faithfulness in our nation. May God grant us the grace to complete what He started with them.

CONTENTS

ACKNOWLEDGMENTS

Special thanks to our precious wives, Michelle and Ceci, and our children, Amanda, Joshua, Sarah and Hannah, for their patience and tireless support. We love you all and thank you for believing in us. Thanks to our parents, siblings, families, spiritual leaders and intercessors whose wisdom and prayers labored to make this book a reality.

PREFACE

On the pages of the book you hold in your hands, we share how the united prayer from yesterday and today can shape the future. In plain words, we describe the lessons we have learned together. For example, we explain some of the spiritual breakthroughs we witnessed on the Kettle Tour of 2001 and during subsequent events. We are not the same as we were before God began to unfold this exciting chapter in our lives, and with this book we hope to plant a seed of change in each reader as well.

This book not only tells a story but also allows you to participate, starting with the prayers at the end of each chapter. We have drawn these prayers mostly from Scripture and note the texts in footnotes. For a fuller understanding, you may want to read the verses as well as the prayers.

We have cowritten this book to give you a larger picture as to how we all can become history makers. For ease of reading, we mostly write in the first person. When Dutch is speaking, his name appears in parentheses after the first pronoun (I, my, etc.) in the section. When the voice shifts to Will, his name appears in parentheses after the first pronoun in the section.

In addition to telling our own story, we have tapped documents that vividly reveal not only historical facts but also the flavor of the times. In particular, we quote the United States Work Project Administration's body of papers called "Born in Slavery: Slave Narratives from the Federal Writers' Project." These volumes were assembled during the presidency of Franklin Delano Roosevelt. Dispatched across the United States to record the stories of former slaves who were still alive at the time, interviewers were specifically assigned to record the accounts in the exact words of these African Americans as a way to retain their genuineness. As a result of and out of respect for the people who lived during the time of slavery, these stories appear here in the authentic parlance.

Chapter 1

KETTLE PRAYERS

And all these, having gained approval through their faith, did not receive what was promised, because God had provided something better for us, so that apart from us they would not be made perfect.
HEBREWS 11:39-40

When God told me (Dutch) to agree in prayer with a dead man, He had my attention! No, I do *not* believe in communicating with the dead—so please, before you toss this book in the trash or file it under Heresies, read on.

While ministering at my alma mater, Christ for the Nations Institute, in Dallas, Texas, I was publicly praying that everything God had purposed for the Bible school would be accomplished. At that moment, I clearly heard the Lord respond to me, "I need you to agree in prayer with the founder of the school, Gordon Lindsey."

My first thought was, *I can't do that, God. He's been dead for 30 years.* The Lord clearly answered me again, "But his prayers are not dead; they're still alive in heaven. And there are things he asked Me for which I promised to give him—things I want to release into the school now. But I cannot do them until this present generation comes into agreement with his prayers. I need the synergy of the ages."[1]

The spiritual-revelation meter in my mind again read "tilt." *What in the world is the "synergy of the ages"?* I wondered, while simultaneously trying to lead an entire student body in prayer, listen for God's direction and process information that made little or no sense to me.

GOD'S SHOCK AND AWE

I am not completely surprised when blindsided by God in this way. In fact, I get a little nervous and quite skeptical when I listen to spiritual leaders who seem to infer that they have the ways and words of God all figured out, and that He never surprises or shocks them. The Bible is filled with examples of God's surprising people with actions, teachings and instructions, both in the Old Testament and the New. I mean, *really*:

- Strike rocks to get water? (See Exod. 17:6.)
- Wash mud from eyes to heal blindness? (See John 9:6-7.)
- Give to get? (See Luke 6:38.)
- Die to live? (See Luke 9:24.)
- Rejoice when persecuted? (See 1 Pet. 4:13.)
- Walk with Jesus on the water? (See Matt. 14:25-29.)

Yes, God can be shocking, and He often uses the unusual to

get our attention. Actually, when we measure our experiences by the ways of God in Scripture, we should be the most disconcerted when He is not challenging our cerebral limits. Frankly, if our God fits a little too neatly into our theological or intellectual box, then we're probably making Him far too human and, in the process, greatly limiting Him in our lives and circumstances— not to mention living pretty boring lives. One thing without dispute is that when Christ showed up on the scene, He blew away just about every paradigm the people had had about God and spiritual matters.

And He enjoyed doing it!

So when God, within 30 seconds, completely stretched my theology, faith and understanding out of shape, I wasn't terribly surprised. Nor was I when those 30 seconds eventually led to my

- carrying a 200-year-old, previously slave-owned, cast-iron kettle across the United States, using it as an altar of intercession;
- washing feet in this kettle, burning letters in it and using it to symbolize the bowls of intercession in Revelation 8;
- adopting two young African-American men as spiritual sons, (one of whom, Will Ford, actually became more like a natural son to me);
- realizing that African-American slaves are my ancestors;
- being adopted into the Crow tribe of native America;
- cowriting, with my African-American "son," a book about all of the above.

Our Theology Is Stretched
Our (Dutch and Will's) God is a mind-stretching, paradigm-shifting, life-altering God! Is yours? We believe that will be your

experience as you read this book. As we explain the aforementioned statements and events—the synergy of the ages, cast-iron prayer kettles, racial connections and amazing prayer journeys—as well as many other fascinating stories and Scriptures, our prayer is that your understanding of God, prayer, healing history and the shaping of the future will expand. You really can be a history maker!

Of course, we are still on our learning journey as well, and we are forever reminded that our understanding and revelation, limited as they are, most often begins from our place of ignorance and hopeless dependence on Him. Having said that, however, it is obvious to us that we have been on a God-ordained journey filled with holy encounters, divine appointments and Spirit-inspired lessons on prayer and the healing of a nation. And we are very excited about sharing all of this with you. Let's begin by introducing the prayer kettle.

THE KETTLE

The first time I (Will) heard Dutch speak was at a conference in Colorado Springs, Colorado. He shared about the above-mentioned time when he spoke at Christ for the Nations, agreed in prayer with past generations and learned about the synergy of the ages. He said, "Not only can we agree in prayer with the person next to us, but we can also agree with the prayers of generations behind us. The prayers of Abraham and the other patriarchs are still alive before God's throne. The same is true of the prayers of those who make up the godly heritage in this nation."

I wept the entire time he spoke. I was reminded of a cast-iron kettle that has been passed down in my family for generations. It is believed to be more than 200 years old. Christian slaves on my father's side of the family in Lake Providence, Louisiana, used the kettle for cooking and for washing clothes. But I have also learned that they used the kettle for prayer. I'll explain about this usage shortly.

My Uncle Willie

A very wicked slave owner, who beat his slaves for any minor offense, owned my ancestors. For example, a story has been passed down about my great-uncle, Willie, who went fishing without permission. The master decided to use Uncle Willie as an example. When Willie returned from fishing, he was tied to a tree. His face, chest and stomach were pressed up against the tree, and his arms and legs were tied together around the other side of it. The slave master then beat Willie with a shredded leather strap that had pieces of rocks, glass and iron attached to it. These, of course, tore away the skin as Willie was beaten. When his beating was finally over, his back bled profusely. Family members placed lard on a sheet to keep the sheet from sticking to his skin and wrapped it around his body. In spite of their efforts, Willie bled to death because of the inhumane treatment of his master.

This same slave master would also beat my ancestors for praying. Slaves were not allowed to pray on his plantation. He assumed they were praying for freedom—and he didn't want them even to consider the possibility or hope of this. Ironically, he wanted his slaves to be Christians, feeling this made them more committed to him and better workers. Part of this was because of what he taught them. He and other slave masters would pervert the gospel and teach, "If you slaves want to go to Heaven, you better obey your master. That is what this Bible says." While we now know that is not what Scripture teaches, it was easy to tell slaves that back then, since it was against the law for slaves to read, and against the law for anyone to teach them (see Col. 3:22).[2]

If the slave master heard them praying, he beat them; but they prayed anyway. Here is where the kettle comes into the story. In spite of the danger, they would sneak into a barn late at night while everyone else was asleep, making sure their prayer meeting was never seen or heard. As they carefully opened the door, they eased into the barn carrying this black cast-iron kettle. Once inside, they turned the kettle upside down so the opening was on the dirt floor of the barn; then they placed four rocks under the rim of the kettle to prop it up and create an opening. They laid on the ground around the kettle, with their mouths close to the opening. The kettle muffled their voices as they prayed through the night.

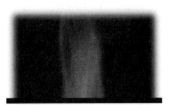

If the slave master heard them praying, he beat them; but they prayed anyway.

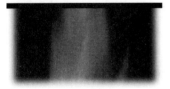

Revelation 5:8 speaks of "bowls full of incense, which are the prayers of the saints" before the throne of God. Revelation 8:3-5 says that at some future point, no doubt when God determines the time is right, He adds His incense and fire to these prayers and throws them to Earth in the form of judgments and power. My family's kettle literally became a bowl of intercession.

One of my family members, who was present in these prayer meetings, passed down the following information along with the kettle:

These slaves were not praying for their freedom at all. They didn't think they would see freedom in their time, so they prayed for the freedom of their children and their children's children.

That absolutely amazes me. They risked their lives to pray for the freedom of their children and the ensuing generations!

The Next Generation
One day, freedom did come. While many of those who prayed did not live to see freedom, their prayers were answered for the next generation. The young girl who passed down these stories attended these prayer meetings until slavery was abolished. As a teenager, she was set free from slavery. Can you imagine being the one who freedom fell upon, having for many years listened to others pray for your freedom? I believe this teenaged girl (unfortunately, no one alive today knows her name) saw fit to pass down this kettle because she knew that not only was she standing on the sacrifice of others' devotion to Christ, but so also was everyone in our family born after her. She was careful to preserve and pass on both the kettle and its history. She passed it to her daughter, Harriet Locket, who passed it to Nora Locket, who passed it to William Ford, Sr., who passed it to William Ford, Jr., who gave it to me, William Ford III.

As Dutch spoke about agreeing with past generations and the synergy of the ages, he pointed out that many promises made to Abraham and other biblical patriarchs were not fulfilled within their lifetimes. The individuals were helping God make history, but the history they were making would not be complete without the work of future generations. Hebrews 11:39-40 speaks of these heroes of faith: "And all these, having gained approval through their faith, *did not receive what was promised,* because God had provided something better for us, so that apart from us they would not be made perfect" (emphasis added).

I know this seems to be contradictory: God made these leaders a promise, yet they did not receive the fulfillment. Again, the explanation is simply that God sees the generations as being much more connected than we do. He may promise a person something and do it through his or her grandchildren, for in His mind, doing it through a person's descendants is doing it for or through him or her. And He doesn't always choose to announce His future timing in advance!

I have begun to see that I am the recipient of answered prayers from centuries ago! This is humbling. But more than that I also have come to realize that the benefits aren't supposed to end with me. I have become part of an amazing historical chain—a generational connection—through which *benefits* are passed on, but so is the *calling*. I'm reaching back to *possess*, but I'm also pressing on to *propagate* and *perpetuate* the process for today and for the future. I'm connecting with history, and through the connection I'm making history. I'm a *recipient*, but hopefully I also become a *resource*. I'm the *answer* to yesterday's prayers, but I'm also a *question*: Will I move the chain forward? This is what Isaac and Jacob did. They connected with Abraham's promises to and from God, reaped the benefits and accepted the responsibility of moving the entire process into the future.

As I began to meditate on these concepts, I thought about the passion God has given me for revival and the heart He has given me for young people. It dawned on me that I could agree with the prayers made underneath my family's kettle by those who had gone before me. I thought, *Lord, I can agree with the prayers of my ancestors for the freedom of both today's generation and future generations in America!* God was showing me in a new way that He is powerful *yesterday, today* and *forever*.

Our Spiritual Bloodline

Here is another amazing revelation: As Christians, because we share the same spiritual bloodline of Christ, we also share the same family history and heritage. I'm not a biological Jew, but I am a son of Abraham (see Gal. 3:7). What an amazing and perspective-altering revelation! No matter what race you are, if you're a believer, then my ancestors and this prayer kettle are a part of your heritage as well as mine. And my ancestors' prayers were for you as well as for me!

African Americans, Native Americans, Asians, Caucasians and all others from the household of faith from long ago all share their godly heritage with us.

Moreover, Christian abolitionists of all races, who suffered ill-treatment because of their stance against slavery, are part of our joint heritage, too. African Americans, Native Americans, Asians, Caucasians and all others from the household of faith from long ago all share their godly heritage with us, whether it be of prayer, revival or a

righteous cause such as abolition. Though it's a bold statement, connecting with this heritage can strengthen our prayers and bring about the healing of our land through revival and societal change.

GREAT AWAKENINGS

Actually, it is not unusual for cultural and societal changes involving justice to be associated with prayer and revival. For example, the prayers of a godly remnant—our forefathers—

prayed into being two of the most powerful revivals in history: the first and second Great Awakenings. If these spiritual awakenings had not occurred, slavery would not have ended in America. God used the prayers of saints of every race and the revival that followed to break the power of slavery. We all share this heritage. I believe God preserved this kettle and its history as a memorial of what happened. Understanding our history is so important!

Karl Marx is often quoted as saying, "If I can steal their history, I can take their nation."[3] How very true! History is relevant today, which is why revisionists exist in America. They know if they can steal America's God-centered heritage, they can steal America from God. Nehemiah was basing his right to rebuild Jerusalem, and no doubt his faith in God's help, on history. When opposed by Sanballat and Tobiah, he answered them by saying, "The God of heaven will give us success. We his servants will start rebuilding, but as for you, you have no share in Jerusalem or any claim or *historic right* to it" (Neh. 2:20, *NIV*; emphasis added).

A friend told me the story of an African-American Christian who was asked to speak at a public school during February, which is Black History month. His subject was to be African-American history in America. Out of fear over separation of church and state issues, at the last minute the school's principal asked the speaker to change the message by taking out all references to God. I was told that this speaker replied, "It would be easier to change the color of my skin than to alter God's record of faithfulness by taking Him out of our history." How true, not only for African Americans, but also for all people in America. We do have a godly historical foundation that is inextricably bound to us because of God's covenant with our forefathers.

Before facing Goliath, David, who later became the king of

Israel, asked, "Is there not a cause?" (1 Sam. 17:29, *KJV*). The word "cause" in this verse could be translated "history." David may have been asking the other Israeli soldiers, "Don't we have a history with God through which He has demonstrated His faithfulness to us? Do we not have a historical, covenantal right to His help? Didn't He say He would fight our battles? Let's connect with our history and deal with this giant."

History is powerful!

Our American Roots

In Hebrew what is *behind* and what is *future* come from the same root, *achar*. To the Hebrew, referencing the future was like an oarsman's way of rowing a boat—they both backed into the future. Everyone who has ever used a rowboat knows that the reference point to keep him or her moving in a straight line is not in the direction he or she is headed, but from where he or she has come. Moses grieved over Israel saying, "You neglected the Rock who begot you, and forgot the God who gave you birth" (Deut. 32:18). The Israelites had lost their historical reference point. The psalmist agreed, saying in essence of Israel, "you forgot your history and it cost you your future" (see Ps. 106:7,13,21).

Unfortunately, as a nation, we too have forgotten our roots. Many Americans have failed to remember the sacrifices of those who have gone before us, turned their backs on the God of their fathers and joined themselves to the idolatry and sin around us. Many look at revival history and say, "That was good, but we don't need it today." Meanwhile, crime and murder rates are out of control. We have gone from healthy family beliefs to fatherless homes and babies having babies. We've moved from the sanctity of life to abortion and euthanasia.

In the midst of all of this decay is a church that has more

money yet less power and influence than ever before. It is one thing to be able to say, "Here is silver and gold" (the Church in America today); it is another thing altogether to be able to say, "Rise and be healed in Jesus' name" (the Early Church, see Acts 3:6). In the past, this nation has seen massive revival. *We need the power of yesterday, today*! This kettle is our reminder that the same God who ended slavery with prayer and revival can change hearts and society once again. He can put an end to a culture of death (suicide, euthanasia, murder and abortion) through another Great Awakening.

So I can pray, "God, remember the people who prayed underneath this kettle. I agree with them in asking for the freedom of this and future generations." Moreover, because of my study of history, I know about the sufferings my ancestors went through and their love for their Savior. God never forgets! If my heart is moved emotionally, what about God's? He can't contain Himself! He pulls out His scrapbook in Heaven, and partly because of my forebearers' prayers and labors, His passions erupt upon the sacrifice and devotion of a new generation today. Agreeing in prayer with our spiritual ancestors sets things in order so that today's blessings can be released—it creates *a synergy of the ages*.

Heroes of Faith

Christians of many races throughout American history understood that freedom is never free. They paid a price, sacrificing their lives for our freedom today. My heart is moved when I remember those like my great-uncle Willie, who was strapped to a tree and beaten to death. I am forever grateful for those who risked their lives to intercede for future generations by praying underneath our family kettle. But, please understand, my heart is even more overwhelmed knowing that they were not alone. I'm sure that your family has stories, too. What is wonderful is that in Christ, my stories are your stories and your stories are mine. Remember, as believers we share the same heritage.

Our collective history is made from a diverse yet unified remnant—great heroes of faith in America, who were passionate for the One who paid the ultimate price for everyone's freedom. Jesus Christ willingly gave His body to be whipped, beaten and strapped to a tree for us all (see Gal. 3:13-14). He not only risked His life, but He also gave His life to intercede so that future generations would be free from the slavery of sin and hell (see Isa. 53:12; Luke 22:37). By accepting His sacrifice as payment for our sins, we become family members who participate in the power of His victorious resurrection (see Rom. 5:6-8; 8:34). As the author and finisher of our faith, by His stripes, He is healing history (see Heb. 12:2; 1 Pet. 2:24). Jesus ever lives to make intercession so that you and I, as His family members, can together shape the future with Him (see Heb. 7:25-26; Rom. 8:17). His prayers for unity and promise of greater works beckon us to agree today with what He started in our forefathers yesterday (see John 17:11; 14:12). Through Him, a new remnant is healing history and making history.

A UNIFIED FORCE

In His providence, God has ordained that we live in this day and time, and He desires that we would add our prayers as incense with the prayers of those who have gone before us. He is tearing down walls, uniting us and synergizing our today with the yesterdays of our spiritual fathers and mothers. The accumulated prayers of previous generations are being downloaded on a generation destined for His glory! Together, let's respond to the call, move the chain forward and be a resource for the future!

This diverse, unified force of believers is also uniting with

God and praying forth His desires for this nation. Together we are shaping the future outcome of a nation as God tips the bowls of another national awakening. We are on the precipice of one of the greatest revivals there has ever been.

The accumulated prayers of previous generations are being downloaded on a generation destined for His glory!

In the first two awakenings of this nation, the human injustice that was pulled down was the bondage of slavery. This time, the bondage of abortion is coming down. In the first awakenings, the false doctrines from the Enlightenment were defeated.[4] This time, humanism, New Age ideologies and witchcraft will be overcome. In the past, God brought an awakening to a few nations. This time He is using our generation to tip the prayer bowls in Heaven and awaken the world!

In this chapter, we (Dutch and Will) have shown how the Lord connected Will with his forefathers' prayers and sacrifice, through the synergy-of-the-ages message. Next, we will see how God had plans to take this revelation to an entirely new level— one that would change both of our lives forever.

*Father, John Quincy Adams said it best when he wrote,
"Posterity—you will never know how much it has cost my generation to preserve your freedom. I hope you make good use of
it."[5] Help us to make good use of what You started in America.
Thank You for those who sacrificed yesterday so that we can*

*have freedom today. Thank You for the sacrifice of Your Son,
who died and rose again and who ever lives to make intercession for us. We thank You that the same God who broke the
power of slavery can break the power of every stronghold in
our day. Connect us with the past revival power that moves the
chain forward for future generations. Unite Your Church!
Make us repairers of the breach, the restorers of many generations. Teach us to pray. In Jesus' name, amen.*[6]

Notes

1. "Synergy of the ages" means experiencing the multiplied blessings of God today, by honoring and coming into agreement with what He did yesterday. See chapter 3 for a full explanation of the concept.

2. Colossians 3:22-25 says, "Slaves, in all things obey those who are your masters on earth, not with external service, as those who merely please men, but with sincerity of heart, fearing the Lord. Whatever you do, do your work heartily, as for the Lord rather than for men, knowing that from the Lord you will receive the reward of the inheritance. It is the Lord Christ whom you serve. For he who does wrong will receive the consequences of the wrong which he has done, and that without partiality." In this letter, the apostle Paul was addressing indentured servants (a form of slavery under which someone becomes a slave for a specific period of time in order to pay a debt, which is radically different from slavery as it was practiced in America). Rather than being a salvation passage, Colossians 3:22-25 deals with the moral conduct between believers in Colosse during the time of Paul's ministry. Taken in context with the other verses of Colossians 3, we can see that he is addressing relationship issues in the church. In Colossians 3:11, he even says there is neither slave nor free in Christ. Because we've surrendered our sinful identity (old self) as Christians, based on our identity in Christ (new self) we are to live out a moral conduct in all our relationships based on whom we belong to and whom we've become. Therefore, between husbands, wives, children, slaves, workers and masters, this is what your conduct will look like. During the time of slavery, Colossians 3:22-25 was twisted and manipulated into a salvation passage, but it does not address salvation. The inheritance mentioned here is the reward believers gain for their faithfulness *after* salvation, not *for* salvation. The last verse related to these relationships is for

masters or slave owners, who are given a harsh reminder in Colossians 4:1. The verse says, "Masters, grant to your slaves justice and fairness, knowing that you too have a Master in heaven." In other words, "Masters, realize that you are slaves to the Divine Master, and you will give an account some day." As evidenced by the Lord's treatment of the unjust master in Luke 12:45, who was severely punished for treating the other slaves badly because he thought his master was delaying His appearing, we see that God did not approve of—nor will He ever approve of—cruel, inhumane treatment, including slavery in America. He desires for all people to be free (see John 8:36).

3. Source unknown.
4. "Enlightenment" is a term used to describe the trends in thought and letters in Europe and the American colonies during the eighteenth century prior to the French Revolution. The Enlightenment marked a key period in the decline of the Church and the growth of modern secularism. For more information on this read *The Light and the Glory,* by Peter Marshall and David Manual.
5. Source unknown.
6. See Hebrews 11: 39-40; Hebrews 7:25; Isaiah 58:12; Luke 11:1; Psalm 78:7.

Chapter 2

PUTTING FEET TO
OUR PRAYERS

*For He Himself is our peace, who made both groups into one and
broke down the barrier of the dividing wall, by abolishing in His flesh
the enmity, which is the Law of commandments contained in
ordinances, so that in Himself He might make the two into
one new man, thus establishing peace.*

EPHESIANS 2:14-15

Connecting with history to make history, plugging into the
power of yesterday today and agreeing in prayer with past generations became more than mere Christian theory for me (Dutch)
when I found myself weeping uncontrollably while washing two
brothers' feet in Will's 200-year-old kettle. My word from God
about agreeing with the prayers of one already in Heaven and
this agreement's producing the synergy of the ages and Will's

powerful revelation about agreeing with his ancestors' prayers under the kettle were about to grow feet. God was about to send us on an amazing journey.

THE JOURNEY BEGINS

I (Will) am a Christian, a husband, a father, a businessman and a spiritual mentor to youth. I have served as a church lay minister for about 15 years. I've been a student of revival, and I have prayed for it for many years. In August 2000, as my hunger for revival began to grow, I felt the Lord calling me into 40 days of fasting and prayer. On the first day of the fast, someone spray-painted my neighbor's car. No one had done this sort of random vandalism in my neighborhood before, so I decided I would prayer walk my neighborhood asking God for protection over it. God began to expand that vision, and before long I was sharing the gospel with neighbors and weeping while praying for revival. I'd take my Bible and declare Scripture promises over my neighborhood, my city of Euless, Texas, and the nation. During this time, I also studied about the first and Second Great Awakenings in America, and I began crying out for another awakening in our land.

At about the same time, my wife, Michelle, had an incredible spiritual encounter. (Actually, I was a little jealous, since I was fasting and she wasn't—just goes to show that it's all about grace, doesn't it?) Michelle had a vision in which she saw a black kettle pour out liquid gold and fire over our house. She was visibly stunned by this experience—so much so that she wouldn't talk about it for a few hours. When she did tell me what she had seen, we didn't know what to make of it—we were hoping it was about money. It wasn't! (Michelle and I often laugh about that now.)

Three Williams

Several months after Michelle had the vision, it began to make sense. In March 2001, Michelle and I were trying to decide between two conferences we wanted to attend. At the last minute, we chose to go to a conference in Colorado Springs, Colorado. The flight we needed was oversold, but 10 passengers didn't show up, so we got the last two seats. We were also the last two people into the conference. The conference was about intercession for the nation, and we thought it would be good to find out what God was doing following the tumultuous presidential election of 2000, and what He was saying about the nation's going forward spiritually. We, however, had no idea what God actually had in store for us.

The speakers at the conference were Dutch Sheets, Lou Engle, Chuck Pierce and Cindy Jacobs. After Lou Engle spoke, there was a ministry time during which Cindy Jacobs prayed for Dutch Sheets and Billy Osten, who at the time was on the staff of Cindy's organization. Suddenly, she began to pray about their going to Williamsburg, Virginia, to do revival prayer meetings. This was interesting, because no one had previously mentioned Williamsburg in the conference. Earlier in the conference, Cindy had heard Dutch share some things about Jamestown and our nation's roots, and the Holy Spirit began to bring Williamsburg to her mind. She stopped praying and said, "I think there is something to this. A lot of people don't know this, but Dutch's real name is William. Dutch is a nickname. [He has since made it part of his legal name.] And, of course, Billy's name is William." Then, knowing that biblically the meaning of names are often symbolic, she asked, "What does 'William' mean?"

No one said anything, so I answered from the back of the

room, "Noble spirit." Dutch spoke up and added that it meant "resolute protector."

Cindy replied, "Okay. It means noble spirit and resolute protector." Looking in my direction, she asked, "Who said that?" There were about 500 people there, but I raised my hand, and she said, "Are you a William too, son? Then come up here—it's too white up here anyway!"

We all laughed momentarily, but by the time I made it up front with the other two, all three of us, William (Dutch) Sheets, William (Billy) Osten and William (Will) Ford III, were in tears. The presence of the Holy Spirit was all over us and it was stated that perhaps all three of us were to go to Williamsburg. Later, Dutch said to me, "Let's pray about it, but I think we are supposed to go to Williamsburg and you're to go with us."

I thought, *OK, this sounds nice. But I'm emotional and you're emotional, and after this conference we'll probably never see each other again.* After all, we had just met. So I said, "OK, we'll pray about it [that's always a nice cop-out], and you give me a call."

A Connection and an Offer

Later, while Dutch spoke, we felt another connection through a teaching he did on synergy and agreement in prayer, which we mentioned in chapter 1. After he spoke, I related to him the history of my family's black kettle, and he asked that I share it with the others at the conference. The last day of the conference, Dutch reiterated that he felt we were to stay in touch about going to Williamsburg, Virginia, though we still had no leading from the Lord as to why.

After we left the conference, Michelle and I prayed concerning this for about two weeks, at which time Michelle decided to look up Williamsburg, Virginia, in the encyclopedia. *The World Book Encyclopedia* said, "Williamsburg, Virginia, is named after

William III of England."[1] *What a coincidence,* she thought. *There were three Williams up there when Cindy prayed; Will was the third William to come forward, and his name is William Ford III.* But the next paragraph really blew her away. It said, "And the Dutch chose William III to be their leader."[2] *What are the odds of that?* she thought. *Back then it was the Dutch and a William III. Now here is William Dutch Sheets asking my William III to go to William's burg!*

A few days after our discovery, we sent an e-mail to Dutch and told him we felt that we were indeed supposed to go to Williamsburg together. We also informed him that my father gave me permission to take our ancestors' prayer kettle, if he would like. I had never met Dutch Sheets, Lou Engle, Billy Osten or Cindy Jacobs before the conference in March, but I sent the e-mail out of obedience and with absolutely no anxiety at all.

I received a reply from Dutch a week later saying that he felt we were to go not only to Williamsburg but also throughout all of New England and the Northeast to pray for revival! Neither of us had ever mentioned New England in our conversations before, but I remembered studying the New England revivals while prayer walking my neighborhood. Had God been preparing me for this? I agreed that I would go, but it still seemed a little strange. I asked myself, *Are we being a little presumptuous and doing this because of a prophetic prayer and what we read in an encyclopedia? It could be some extreme coincidence or something.*

The Itinerary

My remaining doubts were erased a month later when Dutch sent me the list of the cities for the tour. In a very profound way, God truly had prepared me for this prayer journey. I realized that for two years, while prayer walking my neighborhood, I had been prayer walking our projected tour!

First, I noticed that Jamestown, one of the original American settlements, was on the tour list—Jamestown Court was across the street from me. I got in my car, drove around my neighborhood and was dumbfounded. Tears welled up in my eyes, but I was too awestruck to cry as I realized that most of the places on our tour list were names of streets in my neighborhood. This was starting to get a bit wild and strange, but wonderfully and supernaturally so.

We were to go to Princeton University—Princeton Street is two blocks behind me. New Haven, Connecticut, was on the list—New Haven Court is one block down from my house. Also on the tour were Plymouth, Massachusetts—Plymouth Court is across from New Haven Court in my neighborhood; Gettysburg, Pennsylvania—Gettysburg Street is around the corner from me; Dartmouth University—Dartmouth Court is four blocks down from my house; and Hanover, New Hampshire—Hanover Street is right next to Princeton Street.

On it went. We were to visit Williamsburg, Annapolis and Washington, D.C. These cities are in the Chesapeake Bay area, and my house is on Chesapeake Street. Potomac, Warwick, Middlebury, Trenton, Rochester, New Bedford, Nantucket and Saratoga were on Dutch's list—*and* in my neighborhood. Basically, I had been prayer walking cities of New England and America's original settlements—and doing this in Texas, no less! Talk about providence. Acts 17:26-28 says that God "hath made of one blood all nations of men for to dwell on all the face of the earth, *and hath determined the times before appointed, and the bounds of their habitation; That they should seek the Lord, if haply they might feel after him, and find him, though he be not far from every one of us:* For in him we live, and move, and have our being; as certain also of your own poets have said, For we are also his offspring" (*KJV*, emphasis added).

God's Great Plan

Amazing! According to Acts 17:26-28, God, through His providence, knew that I should live in Euless, Texas. He knew a vandal would spray-paint my neighbor's car, and He appointed the grace for me to do a 40-day fast and begin prayer walking. He determined to give me a hunger for revival and a desire to study about the revivalists in New England.

He determined that Michelle and I go to a conference in Colorado Springs, and He appointed us the last two seats on an oversold plane so that we could get there.

He determined that Cindy Jacobs pray for Williamsburg, so He could use her prayer to set up a divine appointment among Dutch, Billy and me. God purposed that I would be born into a family with two other men named William so that I could be William III. He determined that Michelle would read an encyclopedia that said that Williamsburg was

Why would God have all this happen to a white man named Dutch and an African-American man named William III?

named after William III, and He had me be the third William in a prayer line of Williams.

He knew I still wouldn't believe Him, so He determined that I would make the connection between the bounds of my neighborhood in Texas and streets named after places and regions in New England and the Northeast, which just happened to match a list of cities for a tour—a tour, mind you, with people I had never met before and who didn't know where I lived!

Why would God have all this happen to a white man named Dutch and an African-American man named William III? Dutch and I believe that God wanted to use us as a prophetic picture. The Dutch were the first to bring slaves to America in 1619, and William III was one of the first kings to send slave ships here. Now God was leading a William Dutch to take a descendant of slaves (also a William) and the slave family's cooking pot-prayer bowl back to where the evil occurred in order to pray and break curses associated with the land. We were fulfilling what many call a prophetic act.[3]

A Higher Level of Healing

In order to carry the symbolism through to its completion, Dutch told Michelle and me that he wouldn't allow us to pay for anything associated with this prayer journey—not even a soda or a candy bar. He paid for all of our airfares, hotel rooms, meals and incidentals. He said, "The Dutch brought you here for purposes of greed, and God wants to reverse this. So to fully picture this in our prophetic journey, Dutch must pay and you must be served. God wants us to picture and walk out our prayers."

God brought us together and is using our relationship to demonstrate that He wants to bring a new level of healing to America and reverse the effects of yesterday's pain. We claim no exclusivity to this calling—we're sure He is using many—but we are keenly aware that we have a part.

WE MUST BRING THE KETTLE

I (Dutch) remember the strange feeling I had when Will said to me, "Yes, I want to go to Williamsburg with you, and my dad said if we want to we can take the kettle." Will had asked his father about this because of its symbolism of connecting with the prayers of past generations.

Take the kettle? I thought. It had touched my heart powerfully when Will shared the story of the kettle at our conference,
especially the part about agreeing with the prayers of his ancestors for God to intervene on behalf of the next generation. *But
why would we take it with us on our journey to Williamsburg?* I asked
myself.

Yet I felt a very distinct witness in my spirit when he said
this. It was more than a gentle witness; rather, it was a great
excitement—the kind I get when it really is God speaking to me.
And though Will didn't yet know it, in my heart the trip was
expanding to a much bigger assignment. *Lord, You want us to take
this kettle on a prayer journey throughout all the Northeast, don't You?* I
thought. *But why?*

As I prayed and meditated on this for a few days, I felt God
formulating an answer in my thoughts and impressions. "I want
the kettle to represent three things," I believe He was saying.
Though we fully explain them in the following chapter, I am listing them here with a brief explanation of each one.

1. *Re-digging the wells of revival.* Isaac reconnected with his
   inheritance in Genesis 26, and a part of this process
   was digging again the wells of his father, Abraham—
   wells that had been filled in by the Philistines. Like
   Isaac, I knew we were to connect spiritually with
   Will's righteous forefathers by re-digging their "wells"
   of persistent and sacrificial prayer for freedom. For us
   that freedom meant spiritual liberation, resulting in a
   great harvest of souls, even to the point of another
   Great Awakening in America.

2. *The synergy of the ages.* The kettle was to symbolize
   agreement in prayer with our fathers and mothers
   who had partnered with God for the destiny of

America. We were to come into agreement with their prayers, sacrifices and covenants with almighty God. We knew this would result in multiplied power, because connecting with our God-given past empowers us for our God-ordained future.

3. *The bowls of Revelation 5:8 and Revelation 8:3-5.* The kettle was to be a picture of the prayer bowls in Heaven that, according to these verses, are filled with the prayers of God's saints, then mixed with His fire and poured to Earth at the proper time. "This old cast-iron cooking pot caught slaves' prayers for Me," I felt the Lord was saying. "It is precious to Me and symbolizes the prayer bowls before My throne in Heaven."

The Lord assured me that if we obeyed Him and fulfilled this assignment, there would be great breakthrough in New England and parts of the Northeast. The Northeast "gate" (see Ps. 24:7-10) of America had been closed to Him in many ways due to sin and spiritual darkness, but I knew in my heart that we could see a turning in the spirit and an opening of that spiritual gate. He led me to passages of Scripture where John the Baptist was called to prepare the way for His entrance (see Luke 1:16-17) and instructed me, along with a team of intercessors, to do the same.

"Whoa!" I said to the Lord. "I believe I understand these three things clearly, as well as the spiritual principles of forerunning and breakthrough, and I have no problem embracing them personally. But am I supposed to tell people in churches and prayer groups all over the Northeast that an old, cast-iron, slave-owned cooking pot represents the prayer bowls in Heaven? You have to give me some sort of confirmation—a Scripture, perhaps—that I can base this on."

Bowls Before the Altar

I felt that God led me to open my *Strong's Concordance* and look up all the biblical references to pots. Honestly, I didn't even know if there were any. My eyes immediately fell on Zechariah 14:20: "In that day there will be inscribed on the bells of the horses, 'HOLY TO THE LORD.' *And the cooking pots in the LORD's house will be like the bowls before the altar"* (emphasis added).

I couldn't believe my eyes! I verbally shared the verse with Lou Engle, who was visiting me at the time and was considering going on this prayer journey with us. He was as shocked as I was. "That's in the Bible?" he gasped. "Where?" He practically dove into the back seat of my car looking for his briefcase, so he could find his Bible and check it out.

"I've never seen that before," he said after reading it. "Do you think God put that in there just for us?"

"Probably," I said laughing.

I contacted Will and explained this to him. Keep in mind that we barely knew each other. "Will," I asked him, "wouldn't it be just like God, in His irony and justice, to use the age-old prayers of slaves—along with their cooking, washing and prayer pot—as a part of bringing spiritual freedom to a generation of Americans today?" We both were speechless.

The Washing of Feet

Now comes the previously mentioned foot washing. On day two of this prayer journey, we—Will, I and a large team of intercessors—found ourselves in Williamsburg at a place called Middle Plantation. Local intercessors had taken us there, saying they thought it was strategic in our nation's history. When we stepped out of our vehicles, several of my leaders looked at one another in amazement and said, "What is this?!" We sensed such an evil presence that we almost wanted to run. It was one of the most horrible feelings I have ever had.

"This is where the first wall was built to separate the races in America," we were told.

This had been a literal wall, seven miles long, built in the 1600s to keep Native Americans out of a white settlement. There had been fighting and killing so the settlers erected the wall, stationed riflemen along it and instructed them to shoot any Indian who approached it. We are not assigning blame in this situation—injustices and sin occurred in both whites and Native Americans—just explaining what happened here.

We knew we were standing on the ground from which a strongman of division, racism and hatred ruled America.

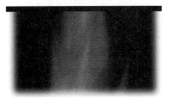

We knew we were standing on the ground from which a strongman of division, racism and hatred ruled America (see Matt. 12:29). There was no doubt in our minds about it. This was where the door had been opened, and this was the place from which he ruled. One of the manifestations of this occurred in the 1940s. This very land became the site of one of the first high schools built in America specifically for the purpose of segregation. It was built to keep blacks out of the white schools in Williamsburg.

"What do we do?" I asked the Lord. "I'm not about to try to deal with this principality unless You give me assurance that we have Your release and instruction to do so."[4] I told the group this as well. Since we were in a private place behind a building and next to a wooded area, I felt the freedom to do whatever was necessary. I told the team, "Let's all prostrate ourselves before the Lord, right here in the grass, and pray until He shows us what to do." As we prayed, I and several team members began to weep in travailing intercession.

After a considerable amount of time, through impressions and Scriptures given to me by others, I began to feel an assurance from the Lord that He was leading us to break the power of this spirit over America and reclaim this land.

You may wonder why we would need a release from the Lord to do this since it obviously would be His will for it to happen. The simple explanation is that there must be an adequate amount of repentance and turning from sin in a place or region before God can bring freedom from the past and heal the land (see 2 Chron. 7:14). After feeling assured that God was leading us to reclaim this stronghold, we received His strategy: "You will break the power of this spirit through humility. You, Will and Jim Chosa, as representatives of three nations, wash one another's feet in the kettle."

The Weight of the Nations

Jim Chosa is a Native American whom God led to accompany us on this prayer journey. He and his wife, Faith, were invaluable assets to us on the tour because of their prophetic and prayer insights, their grasp of history and their ability to represent the First Nation people of the land.

I must tell you that the next hour was probably the most gut-wrenching 60 minutes of my life. God allowed me to feel His broken heart for America and to feel the pain of two large people groups: Native Americans and African Americans. He allowed Jim and Will to experience this deep grief as well, though I'm sure it was different for them.

Each of us was enabled by the Holy Spirit to operate in an incredible revelation that we were not representing ourselves but *nations*. I realize that Native America is actually many nations, but we believe that God was allowing Jim to represent all of Native America. And it certainly felt like we were carrying the weight of nations on our shoulders. As our team of 70 to 80 intercessors stood in the gap with us, we bathed one another's feet, not only with water, but also with our tears.

We gathered bottles of water, placed the kettle in front of a stump we would take turns sitting on and began our impromptu and unorthodox foot washing. The Lord impressed me that we were to begin with Jim—his people had been in this land first. Will and I were to wash his feet in the kettle, with my asking forgiveness for taking their land, stealing their identity and isolating them on reservations. Identificational repentance (identifying with and confessing the sins of our forefathers) is biblical and powerful. Nehemiah, Daniel and others in Scripture did this with powerful results (see Neh. 1:4-11; Dan. 9:1-19).

Through God-inspired decrees (see Job 22:28), we invited Native Americans out of their reservations and into the mainstream of America.[5] We invited them to share in the wealth of this great land and to find their places of influence and authority. We prayed for God's purposes and destiny to be fulfilled in His people, all the while bathing Jim's feet in the kettle.

After Jim graciously received our repentance, prayers and invitations on behalf of Native Americans, we moved on to Will. The Lord impressed upon me that we Caucasians had been the greatest offenders, having made ourselves first in America in every way, and must therefore wash the other two nations' feet first. Jim and I bathed Will's feet, and prayed for African Americans very similarly as we had over Jim for Native America. We repented—mostly myself because of the sin of slavery—and invited African Americans to find their God-ordained destiny in this land, as we bathed Will's feet in the kettle.

Undone by Love and Forgiveness

Then I sat on the stump and put my feet in the kettle. I have no words to express what I felt as my native and black brothers washed my feet in this ancient, cooking, washing and prayer pot, once owned by God-fearing slaves who prayed for the freedom of future generations. As a white man I felt unworthy, humbled and ashamed of our selfishness and pride. I was completely undone by these two brothers' love and forgiveness. They released white America from our injustices and blessed us in the name of Christ. The entire team then declared many portions of Scripture, worshiped and partook of the Lord's Supper together.

As a result of that day, I was forever changed. We mutually recognized a deep work of God's affection for one another's families and people. In my heart Will's slave forefathers and mothers became mine, as did Jim's and Faith's. I claim their righteous heritage and embrace their pain.

ADOPTED INTO THE TRIBE

Several months later, we sensed the Lord's leading us to honor further what He had done that day and model the unity He had intended for the races in this nation. Jim and Faith Chosa felt that the Lord wanted them to adopt me into their family. It would be done formally by Faith's mother, Alma Snell. This would mean I would also be adopted into the Crow tribe. Tribal elders agreed. I heartily accepted and was legally adopted by their family on May 8, 2002, in a powerful ceremony. This adoption means that I am included in the family line of Goes-Ahead, a great Crow leader of whom Faith Chosa is a direct descendant.

Goes-Ahead was an Indian shaman until he had a personal visitation from Jesus Christ who explained the gospel to him.

Seeing Christ was more powerful than any other spirit he had ever encountered, and he forsook his ways as a shaman. Goes-Ahead took all of his shaman material, placed it in three blankets and headed for the river with the tribe following behind him. Fearing the spirits would kill them, the tribe's members begged him to stop. But Goes-Ahead said to them, "Follow me down the Jesus road," and then he threw his shaman material in the river. He led many others to Christ and remained a devout Christian. I am proud of my Crow ancestry.

Then on May 17, 2002, my wife, Ceci, and I adopted Michelle and Will as our spiritual daughter and son. Using the covenantal words of Ruth, I gave Will a coat and a prayer staff, and said, "Your people are my people, your God is my God, and the Lockets who prayed under the kettle—because they were Christians—are my ancestors, too. I embrace the godly heritage of my African-American ancestors."

Will in turn said to me, "Your people are my people and your God is my God. And it's the duty of a son to bring honor to a father, and I will bring honor to you."

Even more overwhelming is the love we have for one another in the Lord. God has given us a genuine love for each other. Will and Michelle truly have become like a son and a daughter to me. Jim and Faith's people are my people—I love them as my own. To paraphrase Chief Tammany's words to William Penn, the Sheetses, Fords and Chosas will live in love with each other as well as our children as long as the creeks and rivers run, and while the sun and moon and stars endure.[6]

A Melting Pot of Freedom

God's intention in bringing different races to this nation wasn't so that they would control each other or destroy each other's identity. This nation was meant to be a melting pot of freedom for all peoples and cultures, becoming one through the blood of Christ. What the Lord is doing through our relationship is manifesting the revelation of the one new man in Christ. Ephesians 2:14-15 says:

> For He Himself is our peace, *who made both groups into one and broke down the barrier of the dividing wall,* by abolishing in His flesh the enmity, which is the Law of commandments contained in ordinances, *so that in Himself He might make the two into one new man,* thus establishing peace (emphasis added).

This nation was meant to be a melting pot of freedom for all peoples and cultures, becoming one through the blood of Christ.

Isn't that awesome! The passage goes on to say, "And might reconcile them both in one body to God through the cross, by it having put to death the enmity" (v. 16).

When we washed each other's feet in the kettle at this wall of division, our hearts were melted together. The bloodline of Jesus removed the dividing wall. Our cry is that God would melt together believers of every tribe in this nation so that Jesus' great prayer of John 17 would be realized in our day and time: "that they may all be one; even as You, Father, are in Me and I in You, that they also may be in Us, so that the world may believe that You sent Me" (John 17:21). More important than what happened to the Sheets, Chosas and Fords, we believe something broke over America that day at Middle Plantation. Through humility, repentance and love, that particular strongman's hold was broken. The oppressive atmosphere of the place was obliter-ated as the ground that had been given to demonic powers was cleansed and reclaimed for Christ. The love of God invaded the area.

THE FRUIT OF HEALING

Not just because of this one incident, but because of the prayers, repentance and efforts of many, we are beginning to see the fruit of healing in our nation. We are not naïve enough to think that there is no longer racial division and tension in America, nor that there will ever be a time this side of Heaven when all racial conflict will disappear. But just as it is with a tree when its root has been cut, causing the fruit to begin to die, we know that an evil tree's root system was cut that day and bad fruit is now dying.

As already stated, we are seeing the beginning of change resulting from God's many orchestrated works of reconciliation and healing. We've observed Native Americans beginning to rise to places of favor in the church, government and business realms. We are aware of the efforts of some in government to work as never before to heal the ancient racial wounds in America. We know personally of high-level government leaders who have knelt before Native Americans and African Americans to ask for their forgiveness. It is a new day—a small beginning, yes, but only above ground. Below the surface, roots are dying and hell is losing its hold. We are thrilled to have played a small part.

In the next chapter we fully explain synergy, the ages, re-digging the wells and Heaven's prayer bowls. Be assured that the synergy of the ages is real. Re-digging wells is both possible and powerful. Heavenly bowls are tipping and African Americans—cooking-pot intercessors—in Heaven's grandstands are rejoicing. So is Goes-Ahead, my new great-grandfather who is sharing his mantle of a forerunner with me.

Come, make history with us as we partner with the God who heals history and saves the day!

Father, we thank You that You are the God of providence.
You truly know our going out and our coming in.
You know what street we live on and how many hairs are on
our heads, and You are determined to reveal Yourself to us.
Jesus, forgive us for erecting walls of division between the
races that Your cross tore down. Heal us and bind us
together in covenant love, and release the revelation of the one
new man in Christ Jesus. God of our forefathers, empower our
future today. Remember Your friend Goes-Ahead and take
this nation down the Jesus road! May a new nation of believers
discard their idols and lead a nation to the river of God. We
cry out and agree with the prayer of Jesus that we would be
one, and Your glory would come, manifesting Your love
through the Church. May it be so confounding that a lost
and dying world would cry out, "What must I do to receive
that love? What must I do to receive that fellowship?
What must I do to be saved?" In Jesus' name, amen.[7]

Notes

1. *World Book Encyclopedia*, s.v. "William III."
2. Ibid.
3. For a complete explanation on prophetic acts, we encourage you to see Dutch Sheets, *Intercessory Prayer* (Ventura, CA: Regal Books, 1996), pp. 35-46.
4. "Principality" comes from the Greek word *arche,* meaning "beginning, government or rule" and is used of supramundane beings who exercise

rule (*Vine's Expository Dictionary of Biblical Words* [Nashville, TN: Thomas Nelson Publishers, 1985]). *Eerdman's Bible Dictionary* (Grand Rapids, MI: William B. Eerdmans Publishing, Co.), 1987, p. 850, says, "A principality is a cosmological power whose authority can work with or against the Lordship of Christ." In Daniel 10:20, we see good and evil angelic principalities warring against each other as a result of Daniel's prayers. Colossians 2:15 says Christ disarmed the rebellious principalities on the cross. Though stripped of authority, they still have power. Territorial in nature, demonic principalities are empowered by freewill agents, humans who willfully sin against God. This may defile the land. Through prayer, repentance and forgiveness, the strongholds that empower these powers can be broken. For more information, read Dutch Sheets, *Intercessory Prayer* (Ventura, CA: Regal Books, 1996), pp. 135-158; C. Peter Wagner, *Confronting the Powers* (Ventura, CA: Regal Books, 1996); and Gregory A. Boyd, *God at War: The Bible and Spiritual Conflict* (Downers Grove, IL: Intervarsity Press, 1997).

5. For a complete explanation on declarations, see Dutch Sheets, *Intercessory Prayer* (Ventura, CA: Regal Books, 1996), pp. 195-214.

6. Chief Tammany, quoted in Randy Woodley, *Living in Color* (Grand Rapids, MI: Chosen Books, 2001), p. 125.

7. See Acts 17:26; Matthew 10:30; Ephesians 2:14 and John 17:22-25.

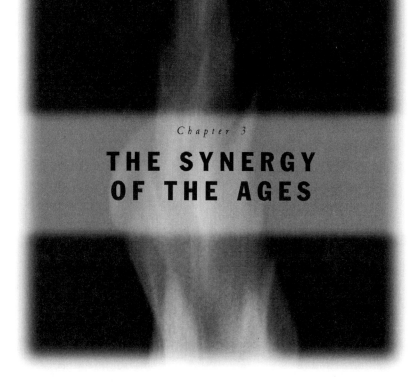

Chapter 3

THE SYNERGY
OF THE AGES

*Behold, how good and how pleasant it is for brothers to dwell together in
unity! It is like the precious oil upon the head, coming down upon the
beard, even Aaron's beard, coming down upon the edge of his robes. It is
like the dew of Hermon coming down upon the mountains of Zion; for
there the LORD commanded the blessing—life forever.*

PSALM 133:1-3

"It's my turn!" "He's sitting in the middle!" "Scoot over!" And
the infamous favorite, "That's mine!!!" Sound familiar? If you
have children, these words probably sound very familiar—that is,
if you're a dad. Moms have the ability to tune out thousands of
miles' and hundreds of decibels' worth of kids screaming and
fussing. It is beyond me (Dutch) how in a deep sleep a mother
can hear a child whimper on the other side of the house and yet

not hear children warring with one another in the back seat of the car. But mothers can. God gave them "selective" hearing.

Dads are the opposite. They can't hear the kids cry in the night, but of course, they can very quickly hear them fuss at one another. This produces great stress for dads. I think it probably has something to do with God's payback to Adam for joining Eve in eating the apple.

I recall one trip years ago when the stress created by listening to the fussing overwhelmed me. I couldn't take it any longer. Ceci was reading a book—yes, through all the noise—while I drove. When I began to twitch, I realized that I was near my breaking point and pulled into a rest stop. Ceci and our small girls, Sarah and Hannah, went inside. Upon their return, they found me on the floor of the car in a fetal position, mumbling something about peace and quiet and not being able to take it anymore. They tranquilized me, and Ceci drove the rest of the journey. She thinks I'm weak; I think she's weird.

THE IMPORTANCE OF UNITY

Children are great, but sometimes they squabble over petty minutia! As parents, we want our children to function in harmony—not just so that we can hear the TV, relax in solace or enjoy our personal tranquility. Well, maybe those are the real reasons, but we know there's a greater reason for unity in our households. Healthy interaction between family members is important to the personal development and identity of each person in the family.

The unity of children has a powerful effect upon their parents, so much so that when mothers and fathers find it, they reward their kids. When our children argue, are selfish or are divisive, we withhold things from them. But when we find them playing together well, respecting one another, sharing with one another and working together, we are pleased and might even join them in whatever they're doing. When they get along well, if they ask us to take them somewhere, buy something or even chase them around the house, we can't help but do it. When our children get along, they can almost command rewards from us as parents.

Father God is much the same way. He is a God of connecting. Family is what He is all about. When He sees His children of different races, ages, beliefs and denominations get along, and especially when they work together, it moves His heart. When He finds us respecting one another, praying and worshiping together, He comes into the midst of where we are (see Matt. 18:19-20). When this happens we can ask of Him and He will give us our requests. On the other hand, when we argue over turf or divide ourselves along race, gender or denominational lines, God restrains His hand of blessing.

According to Psalm 133, unity is the place from which "the LORD commanded the blessing" (v. 3). In order to command a greater measure of this blessing in our day, He is mending relationships among races, generations, genders and denominations. God wants to bring about such a unity in Him that it will make us containers of His glory.

Amazingly, God even established a scientific phenomenon that rewards our unity and agreement. Scientists call it *synergy*. This marvelous principle works in both the natural and the spiritual. In chapter 1, while introducing Will's kettle, we mentioned the synergy of the ages. This was the phrase the Lord first spoke to me at my alma mater, while asking me to agree in prayer with its deceased founder. Though we touched on what this phrase means, we didn't completely define it. We will do that here in this chapter, first focusing on synergy and then discussing "the ages" portion of the phrase.

WHAT IS SYNERGY?

Synergy is the combined action of two or more that produces a greater total effect than the sum of their individual efforts.

In the Natural Realm

If two individuals can each lift 100 pounds, when they join together, they can lift 300 pounds. This is synergy! Charles Simpson once quoted a study that showed that two horses, working together pulling the same load, created so much horsepower that it was as if a third horse had been added.[1] This is synergy, too. Think about it. God established a law dictating that in the natural realm multiplied power would be released through agreement, harmony and unity.

Here's an incredible example of synergy. A man by the name of Herman Oster had a barn floor that was under 29 inches of water because of a rising creek. The Bruno, Nebraska, farmer invited a few friends to a barn raising. He needed to move his entire 17,000-pound barn to a new foundation more than 143 feet away. His son, Mike, devised a ladder work of steel tubing, which he nailed, bolted and welded on the inside and the outside of the barn. Hundreds of handles were attached. After one practice lift—wouldn't you have loved to watch!—344 volunteers slowly walked the barn up a slight incline. In three minutes, the barn was on its new foundation. If 344 people had taken turns trying to move the barn, they would have done nothing but hurt themselves. Yet because they worked together, their strength was multiplied exponentially. If this kind of synergistic power is available in the natural realm, what might the Lord be willing to do for us when we work together spiritually? We could move some serious barns!

In the Spiritual Realm

This principle is true in the spiritual realm as well. For example, there is synergy when we pray together in agreement. In Matthew 18:19-20, Jesus said:

> Again I say to you, that if two of you agree on earth about anything that they may ask, it shall be done for them by My Father who is in heaven. For where two or three have gathered together in My name, I am there in their midst.

He was saying, "If you'll come *together* and *agree* in prayer, I'll join you and produce a holy synergy."

There was synergy available for Israel in the realm of warfare. Leviticus 26:7-8 says:

> But you will chase your enemies and they will fall before you by the sword; five of you will chase a hundred, and a hundred of you will chase ten thousand, and your enemies will fall before you by the sword.

Here God was saying to them, "If you'll fight *together*, I'll multiply your ability to overcome your enemies."

Again, God speaks of synergy occurring when we work together to spread the gospel. Philemon 1:23-24 says, "Epaphras, my fellow prisoner in Christ Jesus, greets you, as do Mark, Aristarchus, Demas, Luke, my fellow workers." The words "fellow workers" are actually the Greek word *sunergos*, from which we get the English word "synergy." This word is used numerous times

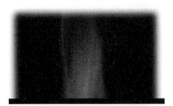

in the New Testament to describe individuals working together for the cause of Christ. Amazing! God is telling us that unified efforts result in multiplied power.

God speaks of synergy occurring when we work together to spread the gospel.

Look at Psalm 133, which also reveals God's inability to resist unity among His people:

> Behold, how good and how pleasant it is for brothers to dwell together in unity! It is like the precious oil upon the head, coming down upon the beard, even Aaron's beard, com-

ing down upon the edge of his robes. It is like the dew of Hermon coming down upon the mountains of Zion; for there the LORD commanded the blessing—life forever.

Verse 1 says that it is good and pleasant when brothers dwell together in unity. The second verse then describes this unity as being like the precious anointing oil that flows from Aaron the high priest's head, to his beard and on to the edges of his robes. In verse 3, this unity becomes a landing strip for the commanded blessing of God.

Good and Precious Fruit

The words "good" in verse 1 and "precious" in verse 2 are the same Hebrew word: *towb*. I suppose one of the reasons translators sometimes use different words to translate the same

Hebrew or Greek word in a passage is to keep from being redundant. Sometimes when they do this, however, the impact is lost. By using this one word to describe both unity (verse 1) and the anointing oil (verse 2), there can be no doubt that God is saying they are more than merely alike or similar. He is showing us that the two are inseparably linked—they function together, harmonizing to create a wonderful synergy.

But there is one more important thing we must understand about this word *towb* if we are to fully understand what is being said. While it does mean "good" and "precious," it also means "fruitful." The psalm quite literally is speaking of *fruit-producing unity* and *fruit-producing anointing oil*. God is saying that just as the anointing of the Holy Spirit is required to produce spiritual fruit, unity among the brethren is also required. In fact, the order in which they're mentioned, as well as the entire context, makes it likely that He is saying the fruitful unity is what causes the fruitful anointing. Beyond being some sort of formula, a heartfelt dwelling place of unity moves Father God to action for His people!

A Blessing in Connecting

Furthermore, in this psalm, Aaron is referred to in his priestly function, which included intercession for Israel. Therefore, we must understand that the dynamic that occurs through our unity is also related to our priestly function as intercessors. When we, the Body of Christ, agree together in our priestly function of prayer, the Father pours out His anointing oil over our Great High Priest, Jesus, and it flows from His head to His beard and on to us, His Body. This releases a synergistic power and a heavenly decreed blessing! You can see why connecting to each other in God's family is such an important part of our personal and corporate success.

If this principle of multiplied power is true when *individuals* agree, is it not also true when *groups* of people agree? Of course it is. We will say much more about this later, but as alluded to in the first two chapters, when through our union in Christ we implement agreement in prayer and action among races, denominations and generations, etc., we will see God's commanded blessing of synergistic, exponential power released. This is what occurred at Middle Plantation where the dividing wall had been (see chapter 2).

Identified as Christians

The beginning of 1 Peter 2:9 says that we "are a chosen race, a royal priesthood, a holy nation, a people for God's own possession." It is amazing enough that He calls us royal priests, but there are two other meaningful words here: "race" and "nation." The word "race" is the Greek word *genos,* which means "kin" and can also be translated "offspring." (Jesus, in Revelation 22:16 uses *genos* to say He is the offspring of David.) The word for "nation" is the Greek word *ethnos,* from which we get our English word "ethnicity." This verse is saying that as Christians we are the offspring of God, making up our own family and race of people. Whether we're red, yellow, black or white, the blood of Jesus connects us. Think about it: *As the spiritual offspring of Father God, we are our own racial identity.*

For example, in my (Will's) case, as a member in the household of faith, before I am an African American, I am a Christian. If another believer is Irish, Hispanic or Italian American, he or she is first and foremost a Christian.[2] And when we, as one new race, agree together in our priestly function of prayer, something powerful happens. God just can't help blessing it!

THE IMPORTANCE OF HISTORY

OK, you may be thinking, *the concept of synergy is pretty easy to understand, but what is* synergy of the ages? Most of us in the Church have insufficient knowledge of how important our history is and how much it affects us.

Perhaps equally as important as connecting horizontally to one another in the Body of Christ is connecting with our heritage—the events that occurred in ages past. We need both *horizontal* and *historical* connections.

We are more bound to our history than we realize—both the good and the bad.

We are, in fact, more bound to our history than we realize—both the good and the bad. Even if we don't consciously and intentionally connect with it, we're still joined to it and affected by it. For example, though we don't often think about it, each one of us, whether we like it

or not, is touched by Adam's sin. We are born with a sin nature because of our human, biological connection to him (see Rom. 5:12,19; 1 Cor. 15:21-22). If today we are connected to the ages that far back, it certainly is no stretch to think we could be influenced by the ages in between.

Sins of Ages Past

As another example, the Scriptures teach that the *iniquity* of a father affects his children three and four generations later (see Deut. 5:9). This doesn't mean that we are judged by God for our father's sin, but that curses reaped from that sin affect the following generations. For instance, we in America reaped a war costing 600,000 American lives—the Civil War—and we are still reaping pain and national struggles because of the sin of slavery.

Of course, we wish we could simply bury sins of ages past and act like they never happened. But try as we may, the fruit often lingers, flowing unchecked into today. We cannot simply disconnect from the fruit of our past by forgetting about it. Even forgiveness of sin does not always equate to an eradication of the consequences. As we shall see later, there is a solution to the sins and pain of our past, but it doesn't come through denial. God doesn't ignore our sinful, painful history, and neither can we.

Our Promise Keeper

However, our purpose in this chapter is not to focus on the negative aspect of our past. We are not only joined to the destructive, sinful portion of our history, but we are also linked to the good. The Scriptures teach that God honors covenants He makes with individuals to a thousand generations (see Deut. 7:9)—in other words, forever. This is why He so often prefaced promises to Isaac, Jacob and later Israelites by mentioning His covenant with Abraham (see Gen. 26:2-5,24; 28:13). He was saying to them, "What I am about to do is not just for you. It is also because of a promise I made to my friend Abraham."

On another occasion, God told King Hezekiah He would protect Jerusalem "for My servant David's sake" (2 Kings 19:34; see also 2 Kings 20:6). Like my forefathers who prayed around the kettle, David was dead, but the covenant and promises of God to him were not. *When we experience the blessing of God today, by honoring and coming into agreement with His promises to believers from yesterday, we're experiencing the synergy of the ages.*

There is an interesting event in the life of Isaac, Abraham's son, where he tapped into the synergy of the ages. In Genesis 26,

Isaac was given a promise from God that his father Abraham's covenantal blessings were now coming to him. One of the first things Isaac did at that point was connect with his past by re-digging some of his father Abraham's wells that had been stopped up by the Philistines:

> Then Isaac dug again the wells of water which had been dug in the days of his father Abraham, for the Philistines had stopped them up after the death of Abraham; and he gave them the same names which his father had given them (Gen. 26:18).

The symbolism here is powerful!

The Past and the Future

This was much more than a man's search for water. It was about a man who was reconnecting with his *past*—the ages—in order to properly connect with his *future*. And God was so pleased with this generational reconnecting that it prompted one of His rare appearances to a human, during which He promised a great future blessing to this early patriarch. In the appearance, God Himself references Isaac's past while blessing his future: "The LORD appeared to him the same night and said, 'I am the God of your father Abraham; do not fear, for I am with you. I will bless you and multiply your descendants *for the sake of My servant Abraham*'" (Gen. 26:24, emphasis added).

When Isaac re-dug the wells of Abraham, he wasn't only looking for water. He was also searching for his identity. And he found it! Basically, the Lord said, "I remember My covenant with your father Abraham. And because you honor him and what I did in his day, I will give you the fruit of that covenant and your own revelation of who I am." So Isaac, after re-digging three wells of his father Abraham, received his own visitation and revelation of God (see Gen. 26:17-25). The synergy of the ages produced provision for his today!

Elisha also understood connecting with the past. "Where is

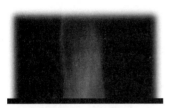

the LORD, the God of Elijah?" he asked, while striking the Jordan River with the mantle Elijah had given him moments before (2 Kings 2:14). Where did he receive the inspiration for such an audacious act? He had just witnessed his mentor and spiritual father, Elijah, dividing the river in this same manner (see 2 Kings 2:8). In essence, he was saying, "Let's see if the God of *yesterday* will become the God of *today*. Perhaps the power I need will flow out of the well of my yesterday."

Connecting with our God-given past is a part of empowering us for our God-ordained future.

And it did!

How does this apply to us? God desires that we today reconnect with the powerful and timeless things He has done in the past, enabling us to build on them rather than always starting over. We can do this individually and also as a nation. He not only wants us to be encouraged by remembering His past faithfulness but also to realize that the promises and anointings released during those seasons are still available today. God's plan is to provide us with a *generational momentum* that comes through allowing Him to connect yesterday, today and tomorrow. He never intends for us to waste what He has accomplished up to this point in time. The lesson is clear: *Connecting with our God-given past is a part of empowering us for our God-ordained future.* It gives us the synergy of the ages.

Momentum of the Generations

In his book *You Have Not Many Fathers*, Mark Hanby points out the generational momentum the Lord wants us to walk in, which was pictured by the priesthood of Israel. He points out that garments in Scripture were symbolic of the spiritual inheritance from father to son, as in the case of Joseph, Elisha and the garments of the priesthood.

In the priesthood, the garments were handed down from generation to generation. Hanby says:

> Garments were created to contain the anointing that was poured down upon Aaron so his sons could also receive the anointing. As the garments were handed down from father to son, the anointing would soak into the fabric. The garment would receive the oil of each high priest, over and over through each passing generation. Saturation would be generationally increased. The anointing was increased, and the fragrance enriched "throughout their generations." . . . In order for the saturation of the generations to be imparted, a priest must wear the garments of his father.[3]

Though America doesn't know it, the nation desperately needs this saturation of the generations. We are much like Isaac, wandering through the wells of history searching for our identity. Since the tragedy of September 11, 2001, we've been looking for heroes and trying to connect with our past. Flags are waving high and national pride is on the rise. But we won't find our identity in patriotism alone. In fact, overemphasizing nationalism could actually lead to a sinful form of pride. God is trying to take us beyond the mere admiration of heroes. He wants to take us past patriotism, even beyond an appropriate love of our founding fathers. He desires to connect us with *the God of* our Christian fathers and their passion for Him. Perhaps as important, He wants to renew with us the covenant promises our forefathers made to God and received from Him in prayer. Will God have mercy on our generation today because we remember the God of our fathers? Can the power of our ancestors' wells of yesterday bring change in our today? Yes!

THE REPAIRER OF HISTORY

This is one way we heal history—becoming a "repairer of the breach" (Isa. 58:12) and of "the desolations of many generations" (Isa. 61:4). We often quote Isaiah 61:1: "The Spirit of the Lord GOD is upon me, because the LORD has anointed me." But the exciting thing is that the chapter goes on to say we will rebuild ruins, raise up former devastations, and repair cities and the desolations of many generations.

In the midst of a needy, desperate culture—which is described in Malachi—all seemed hopeless. But God said, in essence, "I have a plan that will bring healing. I'm going to turn the hearts of the fathers to the children and the children to their fathers so completely that it will ward off the curse from My land" (see Mal. 4:6). Notice that the generational connection, or lack thereof, determined whether blessing or cursing would come to their land.

Fathers and children coming together is more than fathers' playing with their kids, or even two current generations reconnecting heart to heart. That certainly is a part of it. But, as Isaac did with Abraham and Will did with his forefathers, it is also reconnecting with the fathers and mothers *of the past*. God will remove curses and work for the good of a generation that turns back to the personal sacrifices, heart passions and spiritual lives of its forefathers.

Those of us in America are the offspring of powerful founders and revivalists who were in love with God, and this promise in Isaiah 61 is for us. Our forefathers' prayers and devotion dug wonderful wells of freedom and prosperity, and an invitation is being extended to us to re-dig those wells, repairing the breach to His presence and restoring blessing in our day.

It won't happen just because we laud the past or even sincerely appreciate what our forefathers did. Rather, we—like Isaac's, Elisha's and Malachi's generations—must connect and agree with past sacrifices, prayers and passions for God. It's time to take up the mantles of the past, synergize with our ancestors and enter into our own history-making season with God.

However, before we make healthy history, sometimes we must heal some of our unhealthy past. On the Kettle Tour we found ourselves dealing with some fairly diseased history. Yet—as we will see in the next chapter—God has some amazing cures.

Father, thank You for making us members of Your diverse, unified family. As the people of Your possession, we have found our identity in You. Unite our hearts until we arrive at that place where Your commanded blessing comes. Saturate us with an accumulated anointing for revival. Father, pour Your oil over our High Priest, Jesus, and bring a synergistic corporate blessing come upon us. Give us a generational momentum that empowers us to do the greater works He promised. May our God-given history empower our nation for its God-ordained future. Give us the synergy of the ages. In Jesus' name, amen.[4]

Notes

1. Will Ford heard this illustration in a sermon delivered by Charles B. Simpson.

2. We are not saying that God doesn't see color or ethnicity. He created it and loves it. Therefore, He most definitely sees it! He also sees the condition of our hearts when they value our racial identity more than our spiritual identity, which is sin. First John 4:20-21 says, "If someone says, 'I love God,' and hates his brother, he is a liar; for the one who does not love his brother whom he has seen, cannot love God whom he has not seen. And this commandment we have from Him, that the one who loves God should love his brother also." We don't choose the natural family we are born into or our siblings. Neither can we pick our brothers and sisters in Christ. That is why racism is such an ache in the heart of God. It separates us from His family, which is also our family. Moreover, He sees a heart that is pure and loving, one that seeks relationships with brothers and sisters from different races. As His spiritual offspring, when He sees our unity through our family diversity, He commands His blessing there.

3. Mark Hanby, *You Have Not Many Fathers* (Shippensburg, PA: Destiny Image, 1996), pp. 148-149.

4. See 1 Peter 2:9; Psalm 133; 2 Kings 2:9; John 14:12.

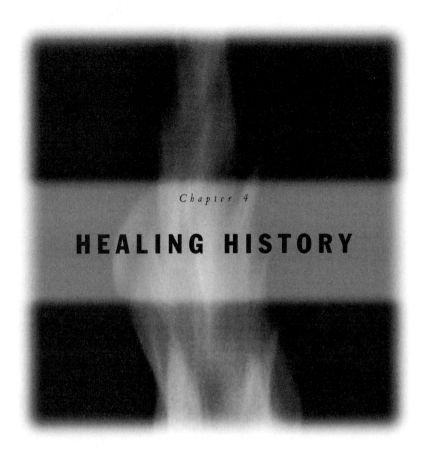

HEALING HISTORY

By faith we understand that the worlds were prepared by the word of God, so that what is seen was not made out of things which are visible.
HEBREWS 11:3

We stood on the ground near Jamestown where many, perhaps all, of the first slaves were brought into America. They were housed in a barn while they were processed and waiting to be sold. The barn is long gone, and in God's unique sense of irony and justice, the land is now a Christian camp owned by African Americans. As we did at Middle Plantation, spoken of in chapter 2, the Kettle Tour group of intercessors asked the Lord, "What should we do here?"

THE REASONS WHY

Before we tell what the leading of the Holy Spirit was, it is probably time we articulate the question some of you are asking: Why was it necessary to do *anything* at this place? Or for that matter, why did we feel the need to do something at Middle Plantation, the place of the foot washing? Was it to bring some emotional healing to the African Americans and Native Americans present? This certainly happened. But if, in order to heal this nation, it is necessary to get every person that is carrying past pain to attend a meeting such as this, we will never accomplish our goal.

Or was the reason, as some might suggest, simply to relieve the consciences of a few Caucasians? You know, we make our apologies, shed a few tears and perhaps give a gift or two, and then everyone leaves feeling better. If that were the motive, it would be pretty selfish. And, of course, a nation could never be healed in this way.

Questions to Ask

As we examine the subject of healing history, the following questions are valid and must be asked:

- Why do we go back years, even centuries, to try to deal with past sins and wounds? Are we simply digging up things better left alone?
- When we perform acts like the foot washing spoken of in chapter 2, and offer repentance to one another, does it actually accomplish anything other than providing some emotional relief?
- Can we or, more accurately, can God through us really heal history? By using the word "heal," we aren't speaking of people simply "getting over it," which is what so

many believe must happen in order for racial and relational issues to be resolved. Rather, we are asking if God can close a door in history so effectively that the pain no longer flows through it. This begs the next question.

• Are there events in our history that become doors—gates, access points, entrances, launching pads—for curses and demonic control or influence to flow to a person or a group of people? On the other hand, does everyone get a fresh start—a clean slate, so to speak—when he or she is born?

So far we have intentionally skirted these issues in this book. We haven't been dodging them, but just allowing them to float gradually from your subconscious to your conscious mind. Our culture, for the most part, including the Church, doesn't address them. Many would actually scoff at the notion that curses or demonic influence can occur based on past wounds or sins.

But shouldn't we stop and ask why, after decades and centuries of trying, members of different races and different cultures still can't get along with each other? Some don't ask the question at all. Others, usually the offenders, believe the offended need simply to forgive and get over it. Those who are the victims often cry out for restitution of some sort, isolate themselves from "the other side" or become indifferent to the past altogether—which is not to be confused with forgiveness. Others, no doubt, truly forgive and thereby are released from the sin and its effects.

This discussion, by the way, doesn't apply only to African Americans, Caucasians and Native Americans. Anywhere we go in the world we'll find members of different cultures who don't get along. Tribes in Africa hate each other. Muslim factions kill one another. White Europeans often can't get along with other white Europeans. British Canadians and French Canadians fuss and fume at each other. Many people hate the Jews. The tension and pain of the Great Crusades is still around centuries after they took place. And on it goes. Why does the pain linger in these relationships? Is it possible that in these cases there is a spiritual poison flowing through history? If so, can it be stopped?

SPIRITUAL ROOTS

We (Dutch and Will) certainly don't have of all the answers, and we would never want to trivialize complex and painful issues with an overly simplistic analysis. But we do believe there are spiritual causes or roots in these situations and that they can be removed through spiritual actions and forces. Simply stated, *yes, God is a healer of history.*

As we briefly mentioned in chapter 2, Scripture does indeed teach that both blessings and curses are passed along generationally (see Exod. 34:7; Num. 14:18; Deut. 7:9-11). The Lord clearly states that the offspring of our bodies, the produce of our ground and the offspring of our livestock can all be blessed or cursed depending on our obedience to the laws of God (see Deut. 28:4,18). That's pretty amazing. If you're a rancher, your livestock is impacted by your obedience to God. If you are a farmer, your land and crops are impacted.

Biblical Examples
Daniel, in his day, knew that he and his fellow countrymen were suffering because his predecessors had "sinned, committed iniquity, acted wickedly and rebelled, even turning aside from

[God's] commandments and ordinances" (Dan. 9:5). Nehemiah knew the same thing. He stated, "We have sinned against You; I and my father's house have sinned" (Neh. 1:6). Though both Daniel and Nehemiah identified with the sins of their forefathers and mothers, repenting in the first person, it was their predecessors who had actually rebelled against God and His laws.

Isaiah 24:5-6 says that our sins pollute the earth and cause curses that devour. Numbers 35:33 says that the shedding of innocent blood defiles the land. Hebrews 12:15, in the New Testament, says that a root of bitterness causes trouble and defiles many. Indeed! Though we don't often make the connection, we live with the fruit.

Generational Flow

Dr. Mark Hanby lists 15 different things that according to Scripture flow from generation to generation. Some are good, some bad. But remember, just because there are negative things that we receive generationally, God wants to cut us off from the bad and heal our history. Here is Hanby's list:

- Iniquity (Exod. 20:5; 34:7, Deut. 5:9)
- Righteousness (Deut. 7:9)
- Illegitimacy (Deut. 23:2)
- Impure heritage (Deut. 23:3)
- Revelation of the Lord (Deut. 29:29)
- Fellowship with the Lord (Exod. 29:42)
- Prayer (As "incense": Ps. 141:2, Exod. 30:8)
- Atonement (Exod. 30:10)
- Rest (Exod. 31:16)
- Anointing (Exod. 30:31; 40:15)
- Offerings (Lev. 6:18; Num. 15:21)

- Requirements for service (Lev. 10:9)
- Disqualification for service (Lev. 21:17; 22:3)
- Financial freedom (Lev. 25:30)
- Garments (Exod. 28:42-43, Num. 15:38)
- Service (Num. 18:23).[1]

Yes, there are doors in history that have opened floodgates of evil and pain that flow from generation to generation. Someone must close them! The problem is that when we try to deal with these roots and their fruit by natural means—legislation, dialogue, material retribution, laws, etc.—we are only dealing with symptoms. *We focus on the fruit and never get to the root.* Though we may trim the tree, there is always the inevitable new growth of foliage and fruit.

There are doors that have opened floodgates of evil and pain that flow from generation to generation. Someone must close them!

Somewhere along the path of history we must get to the root, close the door and stop the flow of self-perpetuating pain and destruction. We must treat the cause. When that door is closed, the societal virus that causes the disease and death can no longer be passed on.

Opportunities: Good and Bad

Ephesians 4:27 says not to give opportunity to the devil. "Devil" comes from the Greek word *diabolos*, which means "one who falsely accuses and divides people without any reason; an accuser or slanderer."[2] It is the term used to describe Satan in

Revelation 12:9-10, where he is also called "the accuser of our brethren."

The word "opportunity" ("place," *KJV*) in Ephesians 4:27 is the Greek word *topos*. You can easily see our English words "topo" and "topography" in this word, and they do originate from it. Literally it is a place, location or a piece of land. Figuratively it also means an opportunity, as this verse says.

Let's put these words back into the context of Ephesians 4:25-32, which is all about relationships. The passage says don't be dishonest; speak truth; deal with your anger; don't steal; be kind with your words; put aside bitterness, anger and malice; be kind; and forgive. Though only a partial summary, this is a very impressive list. It sounds like how people would live in a utopian society.

The Accuser

In the context of this instruction, God reminds us that there is a devil, an "accuser, one who divides," who is always looking for an "opportunity, a piece of ground" that he can take ownership of in order to steal, kill and destroy the people who live there.

Simply stated, our relational sins give Satan legal grounds, a piece of turf from which he can accuse and divide. Until this legal ground is taken away from him through repentance and forgiveness, the pain and division will continue. One of the New Testament words for "forgive" is *apoluo* (see Luke 6:37). The root word *luo* is a term meaning to legally void a contract or pronounce that someone is no longer legally bound to or by something. The *New American Standard* translation of this verse says, "Pardon, and you will be pardoned." When we forgive, we literally issue a pardon, drop the charges, release the offending party and remove Satan's legal right to that division-producing ground.

REALIGNMENT OF THE AGES

Hebrews 11:3 is a verse which, upon close examination, reveals that history is connected and that our past reaches into today: "By faith we understand that the worlds were prepared by the word of God, so that what is seen was not made out of things which are visible." Two words are essential to understand here. "Worlds" is the Greek *aionas*, which literally means "the ages." This verse obviously includes physical creation, but it does so in the sense that it includes everything created within the ages of time. But the word itself, and therefore this verse, is not limited to physical creation. The correct concept is time, or the ages, and all that it contains.

"Prepared" is the word *katartizo*, which means "to put something into its proper position." It is a word used to describe setting a broken bone or popping a dislocated joint back into place. It is the word for alignment and would be the word to describe a chiropractor's realigning a part of the body. Putting these definitions back into the passage, we can see that God aligns and, when necessary, realigns the ages. He not only decreed all of creation and the alignment of the ages of time, "declaring the end from the beginning" (Isa. 46:10), but He also realigns history's dislocations. He heals the breaches. As the Great Chiropractor of Heaven, He adjusts misaligned humanity back into alignment. As the Great Physician, He snaps history's dislocations back into place. Isaiah said He rebuilds, raises up, repairs and restores (see Isa. 58:12).

Down through history, God can be seen keeping things *katartizo*-ed, or realigned. Through blood sacrifices, He snapped humankind back into a covenantal connection with Him. Through covenantal relationships and finding people who would walk in His ways, He kept history on course. Though challenging—even for an omniscient and omnipotent God—and through delays and temporary dislocations, He kept snapping things into place:

- Through blood sacrifice, He snapped Adam and Eve back into place (see Gen. 3:21).
- Through covenant, He adjusted Abraham into place (see Gen. 17:1-8).
- He broke the supplanting, conniving nature off Jacob and popped him into alignment (see Gen. 32:24-28).
- Somehow, through prophets, kings and godly men and women, He kept Israel sufficiently aligned to bring the Messiah through them (see Heb. 1:1-2; 11:1-2).
- 2,000 years ago in Bethlehem, human history received an amazing adjustment back into alignment as God Himself stepped onto the human stage (see Rom. 5:10-14).
- At the Cross and Resurrection, the human race went through the most profound adjustment in history when we were snapped back into alignment with God. Even the earth cracked and popped (literally) when this occurred (see Matt. 27:51,54). The cross of Christ made provision for the healing of the past as well as the future, reaching back to Adam and forward to the end of the ages.

Even though legal provision was made for the realignment of the ages to God's will, the work isn't finished! He is taking humanity down a predecreed path of restoration (see Acts 3:21) toward the *katartizo*-ing of all things. America's history is a part of this. God declared that she would exist for His eternal purposes. And though He knew there would be dislocations and shameful seasons, He decreed healings in the form of revivals, abolitionists and, yes, even a Civil War—for we had to have that painful course correction to realign us.

He decreed George Washington, Jonathan Edwards, Charles Finney, Francis Asbury and Harriet Beecher Stowe. He decreed Abraham Lincoln, William Seymour of the Azusa Street revival in Los Angeles and Martin Luther King. Through them all He was healing and realigning history!

The Role of People

There is another important fact that we desperately need to know and remember: *God heals history through the same instruments that dislocate it—people.* When we confess our sin and repent, even for the sins of past generations—just as Nehemiah, Daniel and others did—cleansing occurs and history's dislocations are healed. Curses are broken and blessing returns. Health instead of pain can then begin to flow through that historical "joint."

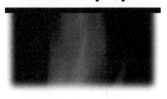

God heals history through the same instruments that dislocate it—people.

Can prayers of repentance and a humble foot washing really play a part in healing a breach in history? Sure they can, when they are done in obedience to God and on the basis of the shed blood of Christ. *History cannot be forgotten, but it can be healed.* Romans 8:28 is the familiar Scripture that says, "And we know that God causes all things to work together for good to those who love God, to those who are called according to His purpose." The personal application, of course, is that God makes failures and successes all work together for good to those who love Him and align with His purposes in Christ. But this application can also be broadened from an individual to a corporate or national level.

The Bigger Picture of Synergy

Interestingly, the words "work together" come from the Greek word *sunergeo*, from which—as we previously noted—we get our English word "synergy"! This means that all of our history, both the bad and the good, can be infused with God's amazing wisdom, purpose and power until only good remains. Like ingredients in a cake, some of which wouldn't taste good by themselves, the bad can be so thoroughly mixed into God's purpose by His sovereign mixer, the Holy Spirit, that all of it becomes synergistically blended into inexplicable good—a good, by the way, that God makes work for His eternal and benevolent purposes.

Through a remnant of people who will repent over their past, pray for one another and prefer one another, God can heal a nation. He can synergize the tragedies with the triumphs, thereby exponentially propelling a country forward into His original plans and purposes for it.

OUR VISIT TO JAMESTOWN

Now, back to the story we started at the beginning of this chapter. What did we do at this "dislocation" near Jamestown where America began perhaps its most disgraceful history, the practice of slavery? Before the Kettle Tour began, I (Dutch) was given an infamous letter written approximately 300 years ago by a man named Willie Lynch. (I don't know for sure, but I can't help but believe his given name was William!) Written to the slave owners in the James River, Virginia, area, it was titled "Let's Make a

Slave." His speech to the slave owners was titled "How to Control the Black Man for at Least 300 Years." No white person I spoke to had heard of the letter, yet almost every black person had. I felt a strong witness that I was to take the letter with me on the tour.

Conceived in hell, this letter was the most insidious piece of literature I've ever seen. It spelled out how to steal the black man's dignity, rob black men of their identity, pit one against another and destroy the family unit, especially by removing the father from the home. One of my dear African-American brothers, Charles Doolittle, who also accompanied us on the Kettle Tour, gave me the letter saying he thought it was significant. Charles said that to this day he saw things in his people that were stated goals of this letter written 300 years ago. It was as though the letter and its teachings had released a cycle of curses that continued still. At the very least it was a blight on our society, and no doubt it was an entry point for demonic curses and influences.

"Lord, what do You want us to do in this place?" we asked. This was always our modus operandi on the tour. We did nothing until we knew we had the leading of the Lord. To my surprise, I clearly heard the Lord say, "Get the Willie Lynch letter, and burn it in the kettle." I felt chills go up and down my spine as I began to envision what the Lord was saying.

There were four pages to this letter. We found four whites in our group who knew they were descendants of slave owners. They each took a page and, one at a time, asked God and our black brothers and sisters for forgiveness. They then prayed that any curses against America, black Americans and white Americans be broken. After doing this, they handed their page to a black representative who forgave them, decreed that the curses were broken, tore the page into small fragments and burned them in the kettle.

I'm sure I don't need to try to convince you of how moved all of us were. Yes, our hearts were broken and our emotions moved upon incredibly. But more important, we could sense things breaking in the spirit realm. A *katartismos* of the ages was occurring! In the place of pain, the peace and presence of God settled.

The gracious African-American owners of the camp, who trusted this mixed-race, kettle-toting mob, were deeply moved as well. They began the time observing—they finished it participating. One of the young ladies in this family has a dream of creating a memorial by building another barn in place of the original, now torn down, that was used to house the first slaves. As she shared her dream, a spontaneous offering began to occur, and the kettle became an offering basket!

Wow! Can God ever write a drama?!

THE POWER OF THE CROSS

Yes, history's breaches can be healed. Each time a representative of Christ's kingdom steps into a breach at the right time and with the right heart and obeys God's strategy, the *aionas* are realigned. The power of the Cross is released, *topos* is retaken, breakthroughs occur and wounds are healed.

May the adjustments continue!

Father, Your Son entered history and changed eternity. Great Physician, heal the dislocations. Forgive us for the breaches we've caused in America. Align us back in place. Heal our nation from the effects of slavery. As only You know how, synergize our failures and our success through Your cross and propel us forward into Your purposes for our country. We thank You that whoever the Son sets free is free indeed. We

agree with the Lockets, and ask for the freedom of ensuing
generations. In Jesus' name, amen.[3]

Notes

1. Mark Hanby, *You Have Not Many Fathers* (Shippensburg, PA: Destiny Image, 1996), pp. 41-42.
2. Spiros Zodhiates, *Hebrew-Greek Key Word Study Bible, New American Standard Bible* (Chattanooga, TN: AMG Publishers, 1977), p. 1821.
3. See Revelation 13:8; Mark 2:17; Romans 8:28; Hebrews 11:3; John 8:36; Psalm 78:6.

Chapter 5

BLACK KETTLE AND THE HEALING OF OUR LAND

*The earth is also polluted by its inhabitants, for they transgressed laws,
violated statutes, broke the everlasting covenant. Therefore, a curse
devours the earth, and those who live in it are held guilty.*
ISAIAH 24:5

*So as to create in Himself one new man from the two, thus making
peace, and that He might reconcile them both to God in one body
through the cross, thereby putting to death the enmity.*
EPHESIANS 2:15-16, *NKJV*

There's an old children's story about a man who made nail stew. He mixed together the various ingredients necessary for the stew: beef, vegetables, seasoning, etc. At the end, he added his secret ingredient: the nail. When his guests ate the stew, they raved about the wonderful taste and how that one nail made the stew better. Of course, the truth is that the blending of all the ingredients in the cooking pot was actually what made the stew so great. The secret ingredient wasn't really the secret; rather, the combination of the beef, vegetables, seasoning and other flavors in the stew was the secret. Any ingredient separate from the others wouldn't have tasted nearly as good.

The United States has been called a melting pot—a country or society in which people of many races and cultures have mingled to form a whole. Attracted by the nail of freedom, people with diverse histories and with diverse ideas have made America a great nation. The blending of different races, cultures, customs, traditions, ideas and ideals adds spice to our existence.

In every good stew, you need to have a good base flavor. While it now is politically incorrect to say this, until recently for the United States that base has been Christ. As a common denominator, He gives our stew its flavor, prevents us from boiling over and serves as the salt that preserves us. He calls believers in this nation to be salt as well. And just as people make stews and soups to bring healing for sickness and comfort from ailments, God is using my (Will's) family kettle as a symbolic melting pot to bring healing to our land. In the last chapter we discussed why personal, corporate and national repentance is necessary, even for the sins of past generations. We shared how this can heal the wounds of history. We will continue to explore this theme here, starting with a story about another black kettle.

BROKEN COVENANTS

Dr. Jay Swallow is a Native American pastor and leader from Oklahoma. He is a member of the Cheyenne Indian nation and is an incredible man of God. Jay is a fifth-generation descendant of one of the most honored chiefs, who was a peacemaker for the Cheyenne. His forefather sought peace with the white man at all costs, working through peace treaties and relationships rather than violence. The chief was well respected around the country— he even received a peace medal from President Abraham Lincoln. He was given a treaty letter and a United States flag; and he was told that wherever he went with this flag no harm would come to him.

For example, on one occasion when Jay's forefather found out that two white women and five children had been captured in a raid by another tribe, he negotiated their release, giving his own food and horses as ransom. Another time, a regiment of 100 United States soldiers fired upon Jay's forefather and a group of 500 Cheyenne. Instead of retaliating, he cried out, "Stop the fighting. Do not make war!" Had he not done this, the 500 or more Cheyenne warriors would have easily destroyed the group of soldiers that they outnumbered.

A Massacre

Seeking a place for his people, Jay's forefather negotiated an agreement to settle at Sand Creek in Colorado. Unknown to him, a rogue colonel and his troops were waiting at this location in order to carry out an early-morning raid upon them. Believing that they were completely safe, the Indians kept no watch. They trusted that the troops would honor the agreement, even protect rather than harm them. But around sunrise, troops descended upon the camp, intending to kill everyone in sight: men, women and children. It actually turned out to be mostly women and children.

Hundreds of Indians were slaughtered for no reason as these soldiers did the unthinkable. Not only were the men castrated, but also pregnant women were stabbed in their stomachs with bayonets, and their aborted babies hoisted in the air for sport. Many Cheyenne were shot as they ran to the United States flag that was supposed to represent their peace and safety. Even after this atrocity, Jay's forefather made two more treaties with the white man, both of which were broken by the United States government.

Four years after Sand Creek, this peacemaker was killed during a massacre along the Washita River in Oklahoma. Before he died, he hid his granddaughter, Jay's great-grandmother, in a hole and covered her with firewood. She peered through holes in the stacked wood and saw her grandfather and others die, murdered by another group of United States soldiers. As one of just a handful of survivors, she passed down the story to Jay and the rest of the tribe.

The name of Jay's ancestor was Chief Black Kettle.

Jay and I had first met during a private prayer meeting about abortion. (Attorney Allen Parker was also present. He was representing Norma McCorvey, the original Roe of the infamous *Roe v. Wade* court case that legalized abortion. Now a Christian, Norma is refiling her case and Parker was soliciting our prayer and input.) To think that Jay and I both have family black-kettle stories that have been passed down from generation to generation is overwhelming. I sat across from Jay in tears as he shared his stories with us—I was shaken and awed by the black-kettle connection. Furthermore, I was convicted with the realization that my generation of African Americans has not been concerned about justice due to Native American people. Jay never mentioned this lack of concern, but the Holy Spirit convicted me as he spoke.

A Request to Forgive

On behalf of African Americans, I asked Jay to forgive me for our lack of care and concern for their issues, and I repented for not valuing or even acknowledging them as a people in this nation. As Jay received my forgiveness, we entered into covenant with each other to work and pray togeth-er until we see revival and healing come in our nation.[1] Our meeting didn't happen by chance. From this sovereign connection with Jay, the Lord brought me much more than an understanding of the Native peo-ple of America (First Nations peo-ple). He gave me a broader awareness of the root issues of abortion in America, which has long been an important issue in my heart. God also showed me how important our First Nations brothers and sisters are in breaking this stronghold and in healing our nation.   .

On behalf of African Americans, I asked Jay to forgive me for our lack of care.

The Call Texas

The same year (2003) that Jay and I met, Dutch and I were to be a part of a prayer gathering in Dallas, Texas—The Call Texas. The areas of focus for The Call Texas ended up being racial reconcil-iation, the judicial system in America and the ending of abor-tion. (*Roe v. Wade* had been filed in Dallas, so we felt that having The Call there was important.) The previous year, a committee had been called together to choose the date and pray concerning The Call Texas. November 22, 2003, or November 29, 2003, had been the options. Our reasoning would have led us to choose November 22 because it was the 40th anniversary of when President John F. Kennedy was assassinated in Dallas, making it a significant date in America's history. But after prayer, a group of 15 leaders agreed that we should have it on November 29.

We knew this date had to be significant, but we didn't know why until after Jay and I met. It turned out that November 29 was the date of the Sand Creek Massacre, and 2003 was the 139th anniversary of this atrocity! One can't help being reminded of Psalm 139, which is pertinent to the abortion issue, saying that we're all "fearfully and wonderfully made" by our Creator, God, whether born or unborn (Ps. 139:14, see also vv. 15-16).

A Link to Abortion

Many believe the first "legalized" abortions happened during this massacre. Could it be that this curse-initiating sin against Native Americans later became a curse to all of us when *Roe v. Wade* was filed in Dallas and the right to an abortion later became law? Through this sovereign date and meeting of The Call, God was confirming to us that Jay and other First Nations leaders were vitally important to what the Lord wanted to accomplish on that day. We sensed that God wanted us, at this prayer gathering, to deal with abortion *as the fruit of all the accumulated injustices in America.*

The Fruit of Injustice

Is this biblical? Could sins of covenant breaking and the shedding of innocent blood really be activating a curse years later? A passage in 2 Samuel 21:1-22 clearly demonstrates that the answer is yes. David and Israel had experienced drought for more than three years. David inquired of the Lord as to why the drought remained. God answered that it was caused by the sins of Israel's former king, Saul. Saul had killed some Gibeonites, a people with whom Israel was in covenant. Years earlier, Joshua had made this covenant with the Gibeonites, but Saul had violated it. This brought a curse upon Israel that was affecting even the next generation. The law that was working here was the sins of the fathers visiting three and four generations.

In *Healing America's Wounds*, John Dawson wrote:

> Many generations previously, Joshua and the elders of Israel had entered into a covenantal alliance with a people named the Gibeonites, and Saul had violated it. Even though the agreement was made without divine sanction, it was binding because it was made in the name of the Lord, and a covenant is a covenant. Saul broke this solemn covenant by slaughtering the Gibeonites. This was a misguided attempt to win God's favor through "ethnic cleansing," an action that violated God's command not to pervert the justice due the alien living among them (Deuteronomy 27:19).[2]

A Bad Covenant Reversed

Terry Wayne Millender, an African-American pastor and evangelist from Washington, D.C., helped bring further understanding to us regarding this issue. He referred to the Book of Amos to make his points:

1. The prophet said in Amos 1:6, "This is what the Lord says: 'For three sins of Gaza, even for four, I will not turn back my wrath. Because she took captive whole communities and sold them to Edom'" (*KJV*). This is what America did in the removal of Africans from their homeland to be slaves in America.

2. Verse 9 of Amos 1 states, "This is what the Lord says:

'For three sins of Tyre, even for four, I will not turn back my wrath. Because she sold whole communities to Edom, disregarding a treaty of brotherhood'" (*KJV*). This verse could certainly be applied, not only to slavery, but to the continual breaking of treaties with Native Americans.

3. Verse 13 then says, "For this is what the Lord says, 'For three sins of Ammon, even for four, I will not turn back my wrath. Because he ripped open the pregnant women of Gilead in order to extend his borders'" (*KJV*). At the Sand Creek Massacre, pregnant Native women were ripped open in the same manner. This verse no doubt speaks of forced abortion. Since *Roe v. Wade*, over 40 million babies have had their lives ripped away by violence in the womb.

4. And finally, Amos 2:4 states, "This is what the Lord says, 'For three sins of Judah, even for four, I will not turn back my wrath. Because they have rejected the law of the Lord and have not kept His decrees, because they have been led astray by false gods, the gods their ancestors followed'" (*KJV*). The courts of America have rejected God's laws, and these judges, along with all of America, will be held accountable.[3]

This passage connected the dots and gave us an agenda for The Call Texas. We were to deal with injustice, the broken covenants in America's history and the covenant we have made with death. Isaiah 28:15 says, "Because you have said, 'We have made a covenant with death, and with Sheol we have made a pact. The overwhelming scourge will not reach us when it passes by, for we have made falsehood our refuge and we have concealed ourselves with deception." Verse 18 goes on to say, "Your covenant with death will be canceled, and your pact with Sheol will not stand." We knew that our assignment at The Call Texas was to break the covenant America has made with death and Sheol.

There were seven national Call events. The one in Dallas was perhaps the most intense and focused prayer gathering of all of them. More than 25,000 people gathered at the Cotton Bowl to fast, worship and pray for 12 hours. The Lord truly used it powerfully. Interestingly, cotton is a symbol to many of slavery and division between social classes and races, but it's also what we use to weave fabric and mend clothing. The Lord redemptively used the Cotton Bowl that day to weave together a coat of many colors made up of all races. It became

God has measured America looking for justice and our nation has come up lacking.

a synergistic, history-healing melting pot and a landing place for the commanded blessing of Psalm 133 in our nation. The Cotton Bowl became a prayer bowl used to produce healing, justice and seeds of revival. Isaiah 28, in verse 19, says, "I will make justice the measuring line and righteousness the level; then hail will sweep away the refuge of lies and the waters will overflow the secret place." John Dawson and Jean Steffenson, along with several Native American leaders and local government officials, gathered on November 29, 1992, and January 14, 1993, at the site of the Sand Creek Massacre to pray for forgiveness, healing and reconciliation. Ten years later, God was allowing the 25,000 present and The Call Texas to connect with what He had started when Dawson and the others had met. God was permitting us to move the chain forward in the healing process. Dutch and I believe God has measured America looking for justice and our nation has come up lacking. But we also believe that a measure of cleansing occurred empowering those at The Call Texas to unite for another level of healing.

A Significant Anniversary

Every year on November 29 Jay Swallow meets with other Sand Creek descendants, but in 2003 he received their blessing to go to The Call and pray for the healing of his people and the nation. In an honest and moving display of brokenness, Jay shared his heart with all 25,000 of us. The stadium became a holy place as he opened his heart and, through many tears, shared the pain of his people. There was no anger or accusation from him—only love. Many of us were also weeping during this holy and anointed time. We will never forget it.

A United States senator came and repented to Jay and other Native American leaders for the 372 broken covenants made to them, and he asked forgiveness for the massacres committed against them. Dutch, representing the state of Colorado, asked Jay for forgiveness concerning Sand Creek. This was the first time that Jay, one of Black Kettle's descendants, has been repented to by state and government representatives on the anniversary of the actual massacre. On behalf of his people, Jay forgave us. He was then powerfully used by God to pray, break the curse of death released against America by his people and decree the ending of abortion in America. Jay and other First Nations leaders were vitally important to what the Lord wanted to accomplish that day.

GOD'S HEART OVER INJUSTICE

Those present at The Call Texas were used not just to break curses over America but also to comfort *God's* heart concerning the issue of justice to the unborn. Is justice really that important to God? Could He really need comfort? Isaiah 59:15-16 gives us the answer:

> Yes, truth is lacking; and he who turns aside from evil makes himself a prey. Now the LORD saw, and it was displeasing in His sight that there was no justice. And He saw that there was no man, and was astonished that there was no one to intercede; then His own arm brought salvation to Him.

Take note of two very important words in these verses: "displeasing" and "astonished." In Hebrew, these words reveal God's heart over injustice. "Displeasing" is the word *raa*, which means "to spoil something by breaking it into pieces." The Hebrew word for astonished is *shamem*, which means "to devastate, to amaze, to stun or to grow numb." Think of it: When the Creator of the universe sees injustice, His heart is broken. He then seeks someone on Earth to share this burden with Him in intercession and bring relief to His heart. When He can't find anyone who is concerned about injustice, He is astonished, stunned and devastated!

Deep Travail

The word "justice" in this verse is *mishpat*, which means "a verdict announced judicially," especially a sentence or formal decree. Whether the lack of justice is legalized racist decrees, such as the Dred Scott decision during slavery and Jim Crow segregation laws, or legalized death decrees, such as abortion or other court injustices, it is God's desire to have intercessors be moved by His heart and through prayer release His kingdom justice on Earth.

This generation must answer the invitation to heal our history by crying out to the God of our fathers.

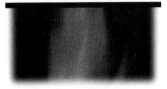

We have experienced what this feels like in intercession. During the Kettle Tour, I (Will) had an experience of deep travail I'll never forget. I wept for more than two hours. While praying and seeking to find out what was happening to me, I heard the Lord say, "William, you walked Me through your neighborhood; now I'm walking you through My neighborhood and sharing with you My heart for America."

With intensity I'd never known before, I wept over the pain and division between the races in America. I then heard the Lord speak to me: "If I heard the whispered prayers of slaves underneath cooking pots, how much more do I hear the silent screams of babies being aborted in America." My heart, like His, was shattered to pieces. Slavery and abortion are both inhumane. In the act of abortion, we kill that for which we once would have died and spurn what others gave their lives to protect—the sanctity of human life. We haven't learned our lesson from history. Consequently, we're breaking God's heart again.

The Synergy of the Races

Fleshly attempts to bring external morality through pharisaical threats and killing abortion doctors have only deafened the ears of society (and we strongly denounce such acts). Converted hearts, on the other hand, will love the unborn. We need another Great Awakening! This generation must answer the invitation to heal our history by crying out to the God of our fathers while we still have time. As demonstrated at The Call Texas, we cannot do it alone—we need each other. We need not only the synergy of the ages, but we also need the synergy of the races.

The importance of synergistic cooperation was made even more real to me by a story that Neigel Bigpond, a Native American pastor, told me:

> My mother was sick in the hospital, and I went to visit her one day. When she opened her eyes, she looked at me and said, "*Nin-zo-de-tow-yoot.*"
>
> "Mother, what does that mean?" I said.
>
> "It means I love you," she replied.
>
> "Oh, Mother, I love you, too."
>
> My mother then responded, "No, son, you don't understand. Our Yuchi word for 'I love you' is not like the English phrase for 'I love you.' 'Nin-zo-de-tow-yoot' means, 'You are like a river that brings me life, and without you I cannot exist.'"[4]

Wow! What an expression—one that expresses how we should feel about one another. Every member, every person in the Body of Christ has a portion of the river of living water flowing from his or her innermost being (see John 7:38). These streams of covenant love converge into "a river whose streams make glad the city of God" (Ps. 46:4), healing past pain while preparing the way for the future. In fact, the nutrients from this river are what bring healing to the nations in Revelation 22:1-2. "Nations" in this passage is the word *ethnos,* which literally means "tribes" or "races." At some point in the future, we are going to see the complete healing of all the races and of all racial strife. But we can see some of it now!

Jesus is our life-giving river, but without the connection of His entire Body, there cannot be a fullness of the river. Without each other, we cannot enjoy the fullness of God's life. The Body of Christ has allowed the enemy to use justice issues to divide us, and God has wanted justice issues to unite us. Instead of pointing fingers of blame, we are to point toward those who need our help. God's chosen fast of Isaiah 58:6-10 says that if we remove the pointing of the finger and destroy the heavy yoke, our light will break forth like the noonday. And when we all fight together, breakthrough for one means breakthrough for all. As root issues are healed, we will see greater results, and fruit will manifest itself.

A NEW HISTORY

One month after The Call Texas, God allowed us to see incredible fruit from our coming together. In December 2003, a businessman bought the site of the Sand Creek Massacre (encompassing 12,500 acres) and donated it to the Cheyenne! They in turn have leased it to the National Park Service, and it is becoming the nation's first national historic site devoted exclusively to commemorating a massacre. One park official said, "We are making history here."[5] She is right. God is healing the Cheyenne people, so now Sand Creek can be a site that is part of healing our nation, not dividing it.

The prayer and the forgiveness at The Call are also affecting the fruit of this tragedy, abortion. A few months later President George W. Bush signed a bill called the Unborn Victims of Violence Act.[6] This law says criminals are held accountable for injury to a pregnant woman and her baby, rightfully recognizing the fetus as a victim. Pregnant women and their fetuses being victimized is exactly what happened at Sand Creek. When we fight together, we can bear fruit together. Our land is being healed. However, this is only the beginning; we must continue pressing in together for synergistic agreement and synergistic results.

It is time for the bride "from every tribe and tongue and people and nation" (Rev. 5:9) to sing a new song. We may not sing it as perfectly as we will in Heaven, but we can sing the song of the unified redeemed.

Nin-zo-de-tow-yoot!

> *Jesus, You are the River who brings us life, and without You and the rest of Your Body, I cannot exist. Break my heart with the things that break Your heart; I want to love what You love and hate what You hate. May justice roll like waters and righteousness like an ever-flowing stream for Native Americans. Continue healing the land of our hearts from the wounds of broken treaties and abortion. Write Your laws on our hearts in this nation, and break every decree of death. Mix our prayers together in Your melting pot of prayer. Tip the bowls and reveal Jesus Christ as the Chief of chiefs and Lord of lords to every tribe and tongue. Cause the living water from all nations and tribes that bear Your name to converge together. Make our cities glad. Nin-zo-de-tow-yoot. In Jesus' name, amen.[7]*

Notes

1. This was not done by the shedding of blood. That is no longer necessary as it has been done at the Cross. However, we agreed to work and pray together until revival comes in America. The words "partner" and

"commitment" don't convey the strength of what occurred. Just as Jonathan and David covenanted together, we did as well.

2. John Dawson, *Healing America's Wounds* (Ventura, CA: Regal Books, 1994), n.p.
3. Terry Millender, The Call Texas planning meeting, June 15, 2003, Anatole Hotel, Dallas, TX.
4. Neigel Bigpond, untitled (sermon, Reversing the Trail of Tears Conference, Ellijay, GA, November 8, 2003).
5. David Kelly, "Soothing the Souls at Last: A National Historic Site Will Commemorate the Place Where 163 Indians Were Massacred in 1864: 'We Will Take Care of the Spirits,' a Chief Says," *Los Angeles Times*, February 10, 2004, n.p.
6. "President Bush Signs Unborn Victims of Violence Act of 2004," *The White House.* http://www.whitehouse.gov/news/releases/2004/04/20040401-3.html (accessed June 4, 2004).
7. See Revelation 22:1-2; Revelation 7:17; Amos 5:24; John 7:38; Revelation 5:8; Psalms 46:4.

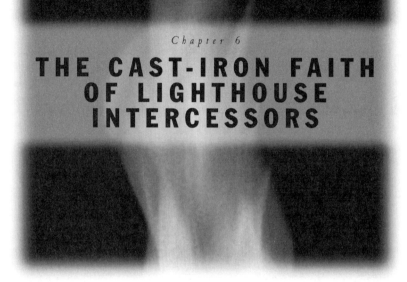

Chapter 6

THE CAST-IRON FAITH
OF LIGHTHOUSE
INTERCESSORS

*But you are a chosen race, a royal priesthood, a holy nation, a people for
God's own possession, so that you may proclaim the excellencies of Him
who has called you out of darkness into His marvelous light.*

1 PETER 2:9

*And the cooking pots in the LORD's house will be like
the bowls before the altar.*

ZECHARIAH 14:20

It can seem absurd to human, and often prideful, minds to let an
invisible God give them direction. And the pride can really be
offended when the direction comes through another human
being. However, God still speaks through praying people, and
the message we ignore may actually come from the Light of the

World. Has God ever used someone else's foolish obedience to confound your wisdom? He's done it to me (Will). This is exactly what happened when an intercessor in Williamsburg, Virginia, approached my wife and me and said:

> Will, I am a "lighthouse intercessor." God has led me to pray for people called to impact the nation with prayer and revival. He uses the symbolism of lighthouses in bringing them to my mind. The Lord told me you're my next one to pray for and that you're like the Cape Hatteras Lighthouse. This lighthouse has black and white spiraling stripes on it. I believe you'll be used like this lighthouse to unite black, white and all races to be a bright light, turning America in the right direction.

I was polite to her, but at first I honestly didn't take it to heart.

Shortly after this happened, I began waking up at 1:11 A.M. God often speaks to me through unusual events like this, so I searched my Bible, wondering if a 1-1-1 Scripture would stand out. But no particular 1-1-1 passage, such as Psalm 111 or Colossians 1:11, made a connection with me. Finally, one morning after another 1:11 A.M. wake-up call from the Lord, Michelle and I prayed, and she said, "Will, get that lighthouse book. I believe God is going to speak to us through it."

CALLED TO BE A LIGHTHOUSE

Someone had given us a new book on American lighthouses. I handed it to Michelle. After she peeled off the wrapping, it fell open to page 111 and an article titled "African-American

Keepers!"[1] This chapter dealt with African Americans in our nation's history who had run lighthouses. I thought incredulously, "Lord, are you waking me up at 1:11 A.M. to direct my attention to page 111 in a book?" He was. Page 111 explained that although it was illegal for him to do so, an African-American slave secretly ran the Cape Hatteras Lighthouse, the same lighthouse that the lighthouse intercessor said I represented! Michelle and I were a bit undone and, yes, I was again humbled. God was shining His light on those who had moved His heart in the past, and through them He was leading us down an unusual path.

But God wasn't finished confirming this unique picture of my calling. A few weeks later, I went to a preservice prayer time at an African-American congregation. The elders gathered at the front, knelt down and began to sing very slowly, "Let the Light of the Lighthouse Shine on Me!" When they were finished, I asked about this song, and I was told that it's an old Negro slave spiritual that was used by Harriet Tubman and others as a code song during slavery. When "Lighthouse" was sung, it alerted slaves working that day to a rescue that night by Tubman and others working on the Underground Railroad. In the dark of night, a flashing light, created by a mirror reflecting the light of the moon, would lead runaway slaves. Black and white Christians worked together on the Underground Railroad and set many captives free. They were the original unified, black and white *lighthouse intercessors*.

First Peter 2:9, a Scripture we referenced earlier, speaks of our unity and priestly function of prayer as believers. The last portion of this Scripture, along with saying we're a chosen race of priests, says, we "proclaim the excellencies of Him who has called [us] *out of darkness into His marvelous light*" (emphasis added). The word "light" is *phos*, which means, "to shine or make manifest, especially by rays." As a unified royal priesthood, we live in the light; and as intercessors we pierce the darkness of our day by manifesting God's light through intercession. Sounds like a spiritual version of the Cape Hatteras Lighthouse, doesn't it?

What happened to me is really about all of us. Like the Cape Hatteras Lighthouse, the Lord is calling blacks, whites and people of all races to unite in prayer to turn our nation in the right direction. A new lighthouse is being erected that will guide those bound by the enemy, moving them "out of darkness into His marvelous light."

THE GENERATIONS CONNECTED

In the last few chapters we discussed the need to break *curses* flowing from the past into the present. But generational *blessings* are also powerful and available. In this chapter we want to connect with the hidden legacy of prayer and intercession from Christian slaves and abolitionists. You'll see their heart passions and sacrifice. Through this, you'll gain a better understanding of how intercession is not only about prayer but also about being a mediator who is actively involved in releasing the will of Heaven on Earth. This is exactly what Christian "lighthouses" did generations ago during the time of slavery. Let's look at how brotherly love, prayer and sacrifice changed the nation.

As we mentioned before, my ancestor's kettle was used by the Lord as a reminder of the prayer bowls in heaven. God gave Zechariah 14:20 to Dutch. It says, "The *cooking pots* in the LORD'S house will be like the *bowls* before the altar" (emphasis added). This old kettle in my family caught the muffled prayers of slaves in the same way that bowls in Heaven catch the incense of our prayers (see Rev. 5:8).

More Cast-Iron Kettles

Before Dutch and I began writing, however, I made a most remarkable discovery. Praying under a kettle wasn't isolated to just my family. According to Albert J. Raboteau, professor of religion at Princeton University, slaves often used kettles to conceal their prayer meetings:

> The most common device for preserving secrecy was an iron pot usually placed in the middle of the cabin floor or at the doorstep, then slightly propped up to hold the sound of the praying and singing from escaping. A variation was to pray or sing softly "with heads together around" the "kettle to deaden the sound."[2]

This discovery led me to a study of slave narratives from across the country. I learned that like my ancestors a remnant of Christian slaves on plantations had also used kettles and other containers to conceal their prayer meetings. Laura Thornton, a former slave from Arkansas, said:

> Ole boss wold tie em tuh a tree and whoop em if dey caught us even praying. We had er big black washpot an de way we prayed we'd go out an put our mouths to der groun and pray low and de sound wud go up under de pot an ole boss couldn't hear us.[3]

Former slave Alex Woods of North Carolina recalled:

> Dey would not allow us to have prayer meetings in our houses, but we would gather late in de night and turn

pots upside down inside de door to kill de sound and sing and pray for freedom. No one could hear unless dey eaves-drapped.[4]

Lucretia Alexander, a young girl during slavery, described her father and older slaves on the plantation as Christians. She confirmed that they turned the pots down to pray and "they used to sing their songs in a whisper and pray in a whisper. That was a prayer-meeting from house to house once or twice—once or twice a week."[5]

Because of the danger, the slaves who prayed under pots appointed lookouts to alert them if the master or his overseers were coming. As the lookouts watched, others prayed, using barrels, iron wash pots and cooking kettles to muffle their voices. In her narrative, Kitty Hill recounted:

Dey turned pots down ter kill de noise an' held meetings at night. Dey had [slaves] ter watch an' give de alarm if dey saw de [overseers]. Dey always looked out for [patrollers]."[6]

When asked why they used this method to conceal their voices, one former slave replied, "I don't know where they learned to do that. I kinda think the Lord put them things in their minds to do for themselves, just like he helps us Christians in other ways. Don't you think so?"[7] At times, praying under a kettle could not contain their fervent love for Christ.

A great story comes from former Mississippi slave Edd Roby. He tells how one woman was praying under a pot and got full of o' 'ligion, or religion.[8] In other words, the Holy Spirit came upon her and she burst forth in such an exuberant worship that no kettle could contain it! Her marsa (master) and missus (master's wife) came to stop the tumult, but God had something else in mind. Roby remembered:

> One day dis old woman was a prayin' in de pot an' got so full o' 'ligion 'till she got her head out dat pot an' was jus' a tellin' de news. Old Missus heard her an' went to see what was de matter. Missus, she got happy an' finally Marsa heard 'em an' went to see what de trouble was. Marsa, he got full o' 'ligion too an' dey all had a big time. After dat day dey said dey never did whip 'em fo' prayin' no more.[9]

This remarkable account shows how God used the prayers of this slave to set her masters spiritually free.

Of course, other slaves had different outcomes. Yet regardless of the consequences, they prayed anyway. Like the stories passed down in our family, many Christian slave narratives show how their ancestors yearned to hold underground gatherings because they wanted to pray for freedom and desired more of God. Candus Richardson reported that her friend's husband, a very pious man, was often beaten because he would "steal off to the woods and pray . . . but the beatings never stopped him from praying. . . . Her husband was very religious. He just kept on praying. One time, [master] beat her husband so unmerciful for praying that his shirt was as red from blood stain as if you'd paint it with a brush."[10] Her claim is true: "It was his prayers and a whole lot of other slaves that cause you young folks to be free today."[11]

The incredible accounts of these intercessors show the depth of their love for God. They risked their lives to spend quality, intimate time with their supreme master, Jesus Christ. The embrace they felt from His presence was worth risking their very lives. We can connect to and build upon this legacy.

Holy Tabernacles

Slaves also concealed prayer meetings by building temporary tabernacles, called brush harbors or hush harbors. In the dark of night, those first to the selected spot bent the boughs of trees as they walked along in the direction of the prayer meeting. Those following behind felt which direction these branches were bent, which guided them to the prayer meeting. After arriving in the desired location, they soaked quilts with water, which were used to build four walls around them. This created a tabernacle. The wet blankets helped to deaden the sound as they prayed.[12]

Slaves risked their lives to spend quality, intimate time with their supreme master, Jesus Christ.

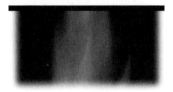

The prayer life of these slaves was incredible. In the following excerpt an anonymous slave intercedes, starting by referencing Psalm 137:1-4. He or she then makes entreaty for the Civil War and freedom and ends by praying for ensuing generations:

> Masser Jesus, like de people ob de ole time, de Jews, we weep by the side ob de ribber, wid de srings ob de harp all broken. But we sing ob de broken heart, as dem people could not do so. Hear us King, in our present state of sorrows. . . . Help us for our own good, and de good ob God's blessed Union people, dat want all people free, whatsomebedder de color. . . . Master Jesus, you know

de deep tribulation ob our hearts, dat our children dying in de camp, and as we tote dem from one place to tudder, and bury dem in de cold ground, Jesus, to go in spirit, to de God of de people whare de soul hab no spot nor color. Great King ob Kings, and Doctor ob Doctors, and God ob Battles, help us to be well. Help us to be able to fight wid de Union sogers de battle for de Union—help us to fight for liberty—fight for de country—fight for our homes, and our own free children, and our children's children.[13]

Tom Robinson from Arkansas was sold three times before his 15th birthday and was taken across America. As a result he was separated from his mother at an early age. After gaining his freedom, Robinson said his only memory was of his mother praying for everyone's freedom. He says, "There she was a'praying, and on other plantations women was a'praying. All over the country the same prayer was prayed. Guess the Lord done heard the prayer and answered it."[14]

The Power of Prayer

Prayers offered in secret, wet-blanket tabernacles and muffled under cast-iron kettles filled golden prayer bowls in Heaven! It's exciting to think that our prayers are stored in the same place. Note that in Revelation 5:8, "bowls" is plural. We don't know how many bowls hold our prayers, but I think it's very likely that each of us has his or her own bowl in Heaven. I don't know if they are literal or symbolic, and it doesn't matter. The principle is still the same—God stores our prayers for use at the proper time. It is awesome to think our prayers go up to Heaven as incense and are collected inside bowls before God's altar. At the right time, God turns these bowls over and pours out a powerful release in answer to prayer:

And another angel came and stood over the altar, having a golden censer; and there was given unto him much incense, that he should add it unto the prayers of all the saints upon the golden altar which was before the throne. And the smoke of the incense, with the prayers of the saints, went up before God out of the angel's hand. And the angel taketh the censer; and he filled it with the fire of the altar, and cast it upon the earth: and there followed thunders, and voices, and lightnings, and an earthquake (Rev. 8:3-5, *ASV*).

That's incredible! The part I like most is that God adds "much incense" to the incense caused by our prayers. Where does the added incense come from? Is it the Holy Spirit's groans of Romans 8:26-27; the intercession of others around the world (past or present); or Jesus, our Great High Priest? I'm not sure—and, quite frankly, it could be all three. The beauty is that when we pray we are privileged to partner with God's eternal purposes. He releases the answer to our prayers either when He knows it is the right time to do something or when enough prayer has accumulated to get the job done.

This passage also says that God takes the prayers in our bowl and mixes them with fire from Heaven's altar. Picture this: God takes the same fire that fell on Sinai; the fire that consumed the sacrifice, rocks and water when Elijah was on the mountain; the fire that fell at Pentecost; the fire that destroys His enemies—the fire of God Almighty—and He mixes our bowl of prayers with it! Then He pours the contents of the bowl upon the earth. In the spiritual realm, lightning starts to flash, thunder crashes, and the earth quakes. This release of power in the spirit realm provides results in the natural realm.

GREAT AWAKENINGS

The prayers of God's people in America have produced two Great Awakenings, one in the 1730-1740 era and another in the 1840-1860 time frame. Whispered prayers on Earth were turned into precious incense, becoming shouts and loud cries in Heaven. God determined when the right time would be; then handed much incense to an angel who mixed it with fire from the altar. Thunder, fire, lightning and earthquakes were hurled to Earth and revivals shook America in these two Great Awakenings.

In these outpourings, God's presence wasn't confined to a church building; rather, it spread over entire cities and regions. People received healings of all kinds. Men in pubs wept on their barstools, and people in the streets were convicted of their sins. These revivals were so powerful that they transformed the culture.

Whispered prayers on Earth were turned into precious incense, becoming shouts and loud cries in Heaven.

An interesting irony concerning these two moves of God's spirit is that both preceded major wars for freedom. The first one occurred before the Revolutionary War, a war in which an oppressed people sought to win their God-given right to life, liberty and the pursuit of happiness. In it settlers were freed—but slaves weren't.

The irony of the Second Great Awakening is that in the place where slavery thrived in America, a move of the Holy Spirit helped birth and greatly fueled the abolition movement, an attempt to rid the nation of slavery. Eventually these people in the North were willing to lay their lives down for this cause. The American Civil War was God's tragic solution to an insidious injustice, and in some ways it was born of a great outpouring of His Spirit.

Even in God's wrath, he was remembering mercy (see Hab. 3:2). A great revival preceded the judgment, prepared a nation for war, helped turn injustice into justice and freed another generation of Americans. I know of no other nation that has survived a civil war of the magnitude we experienced. There was, indeed, much mercy interlaced with great judgment.

Slavery, the human injustice leading up to the second Awakening and the Civil War came to an end because a godly remnant of people, united in intercession and made one by the blood of Christ, worked together in a synergy-creating agreement. A lighthouse of prayer, made up of black and white intercessors, was erected and turned a nation, preserving it from a fatal, destiny-robbing collision with the rocks of injustice. Quiet but fervent prayers for freedom offered underneath kettles, joined with the prayers and sermons of a Great Awakening, were answered. One day God tipped over their prayer bowls in Heaven and changed society.

Some translations of Revelation 8:5 say that when these prayer bowls are poured upon Earth, they release "voices" (*KJV, ASV*). Revivalists and abolitionists were voices for the voiceless and became answers to secret prayers. They became intercessory mediators who spoke out, risking their lives for the freedom of others. And like Abel, though they are dead, they're still speaking (see Heb. 11:4). We can connect with their righteous hearts, prayers and sacrifice, and see another freedom-causing awakening today.

One of those voices, the white abolitionist Elijah P. Lovejoy, was a martyr's voice, killed for preaching against slavery. His last speech was an appeal before his city council for protection from mobs that had damaged his printing press because he print- ed abolitionist material. The council members told him he wouldn't have any trouble if he stopped preaching against slav- ery. Here is his reply:

> I have counted the cost, and stand prepared freely to offer up my all in the service to God. Yes, sir, I am fully aware of all the sacrifice I make, in here pledging myself to continue this contest to the last. (Forgive these tears— I had not intended to shed them, and they flow not for myself but for others). . . . The time for fulfilling this pledge in my case, it seems to me, has come. Sir, I dare not flee away from Alton. Should I attempt it, I should feel that the angel of the Lord, with his flaming sword, was pursuing me wherever I went. It is because I fear God that I am not afraid of all who oppose me in this city. . . . Before God and you all, I here pledge myself to continue it, if need be, till death. If I fall, my grave shall be made in Alton.[15]

His determined decree proved to be prophetic. Lovejoy's printing press was torn down because of his stand against slav- ery, and he rebuilt it three times. When he tried to rebuild it a fourth time, it cost him his life. His house was set on fire, and as he ran out to escape the flames, he was shot by the mob that was waiting for him outside. He and others like him make up a mul- tiracial, godly remnant who prayed, preached and sacrificed, tak- ing their stand against the human injustice of their day. Like Moses, they chose to suffer with the people of God rather than compromise and wink at the sin of slavery (see Heb. 11:25-27).

History is powerful. But we're not called only to be history rememberers—we're called to also be history makers. We can build on our godly heritage. Yes, at times the past gives us reason to fear, but it also gives us reason to believe. God wants us to know that the same revival power that was available to people yesterday is present for us today. Many people in the 1700s and 1800s did their part praying for revival and the healing of this nation. Now our generation is being given an invitation to write our own history. Our prayers and actions are the pen, and our legacy as a nation is being determined by the decisions we're making today. If written now, our epitaph would have to say that we were weighed in the balance and found wanting. Our condition is critical.

William Booth, founder of the Salvation Army, speaking of our day said, "Six things will dominate young people at the turn of the century: Religion without the Holy Spirit; forgiveness without repentance; conversion without the new birth; Christianity without Christ; politics without God; and Heaven without hell."[16]

Was he accurate? Yes, but it isn't only young people who fit the description. Consider the following facts about our nation:

- 1998 brought about no change in the percentage of adults who are born-again Christians.
- When compared to statistics for 1991, church attendance and Bible reading are at lower levels of involvement. (This means we have actually lost ground.)
- Six out of 10 Americans (61 percent) agree that "the Holy Spirit is a symbol of God's presence or power but is not a living entity."
- A majority (55 percent) of all born-again Christians reject the existence of the Holy Spirit.
- One out of every five born-again Christians believes

that the Bible contains errors.

- Only 44 percent of born-again Christians are very certain of the absoluteness of moral truth.
- Rather than following Jesus' exhortation to be in the world but not of it, today's Christians seem to thirst for the opposite reality—to be inseparable from the world, while somehow retaining the aura of devout followers of Christ.[17]

We need the cast-iron faith of our forefathers. Peter Marshall and David Manuel write about the destiny, history and current condition of America in *Sounding Forth the Trumpet*. They make the point that it is not too late for America:

> Today, if we turn back to God and seek His face and turn from our wicked ways, we will experience a similar revival. Hopefully it will reverse our downward slide into a new Dark Age. Even if it does not, it will prepare us for what we must go through.[18]

We agree that there is still time for America. God doesn't release His divine judgment until He has fully exhausted His divine mercy. It is not too late for us as a nation to turn back to God. The story is told of a ship captain who saw lights ahead on a dark night and told his radioman to send a message to these lights:

> "Alter your course, ten degrees south."
> The reply came back, "Alter your course ten degrees north."
> The captain grew angry. Who would dare deny his commands? Utilizing his rank, he sent the message,

"Alter your course ten degrees south; I am the captain!"

The reply came back, "Alter your course ten degrees
north; I am Seaman 3rd Class Jones."

The captain, knowing what fear it would evoke, sent the
intimidating message, "Alter your course, ten
degrees south; I am a battleship!"

The reply came back, "Alter your course ten degrees
north. I am a lighthouse."

In the midst of dark and foggy times when lines are blurred,
good is called evil and evil, good. We cannot allow our prideful
minds to miss the direction of an invisible God. Through prayer
and action we must be lighthouse intercessors, shining His light
and piercing the darkness of deception. We don't have to blind
others with its strength—if we release the light God's way, it will
guide them. God's desire is to bring all of the parts in the Body
of Christ together to shed His light on America and guide it in
the right direction. God is extending to us an invitation to tip
prayer bowls over our family, neighborhood, city and nation.
Angels are standing at attention, waiting for our incense, so that
they can add it to the prayers of other saints. The synergy of our
prayers will erect a lighthouse that affects national destinies, sets
captives free and turns millions to the Light of the World.
Speaking in Senegal, President George W. Bush, in a powerful
speech on the subject of American slavery, said:

In America, enslaved Africans learned the story of the exodus from Egypt and set their own hearts on a promised
land of freedom. Enslaved Africans discovered a suffering
Savior and found he was more like themselves than their
masters. Enslaved Africans heard the ringing promises of

the Declaration of Independence and asked the self-evident question, "Then why not me?" That deliverance was demanded by escaped slaves named Frederick Douglas and Sojourner Truth . . . Booker T. Washington . . . and ministers of the gospel named Leon Sullivan and Martin Luther King, Jr. . . . We can discern eternal standards in the deeds of William Wilberforce and John Quincy Adams and Harriet Beecher Stowe, and Abraham Lincoln. These men and women, black and white, burned with a zeal for freedom, and they left behind a different and better nation. Their moral vision caused Americans to examine our hearts, to correct our Constitution, and to teach our children the dignity and equality

Through prayer and action we must be lighthouse intercessors, shining His light and piercing the darkness of deception.

of every person of every race. By a plan known only to Providence, the stolen sons and daughters of Africa helped to awaken the conscience of America. The very people traded into slavery helped to set America free.[19]

These bold and powerful words of President Bush bring light to the irony of an enslaved people's bringing freedom and justice to America. As a nation we're in need of freedom again. We need a society-changing revival that frees America from the chains of sin. Think about it. Wouldn't it be like God, in His justice and irony, to remember the prayers of a slave generation, mix them with ours and free a nation once again through another powerful great awakening?

Please, Lord, tip the bowls!

*Light of the World, turn our nation in the right direction. Raise
up a lighthouse of prayer with believers of all races who will
shine brightly in dark places and be voices for the voiceless. Give
us the cast-iron faith to believe, to fight, to pray, to war for You
and our nation. Father, remember the prayers of Your Son and
those who have been devoted to Him. Remember their
sacrifices, and tip the bowls of prayer over America again.
Release Your thunder, fire, lightning and earthquakes! Come
with Your earthquakes and shake everything from the Church
to government to the marketplace with another awakening.
Release Your lightning and shock us into the reality of our desperate need for You. Let Your fire come and ignite a fiery,
loving desire for Jesus Christ! Bring the fear of the Lord and
holiness back in Your Church. Send another awakening, oh,
God! In Jesus' name, so be it.[20]*

Notes

1. F. Ross Holland, *Lighthouses* (New York: Barnes and Noble Books, 1995), p. 111.
2. Albert J. Raboteau, *Slave Religion: The Invisible Institution in the Antebellum South* (New York: Oxford University Press, 1978), p. 215. Frightened of slave uprisings, slave masters did not allow separate gatherings. They also feared that praying slaves created hope for freedom, building their courage to run away. As a result, slave church services and prayer meetings were strictly forbidden. Disobeying these rules brought brutal punishment. Many slaves heard the gospel by attending white church services. Some said they could only listen from a window on the outside of the church. Others said they were allowed inside but sat in separate sections from whites. Many slaves became ministers but didn't have the freedom to minister without oversight by the master. Some masters provided church

services for them, but according to ex–Texas slave William Mathews, "Colored preachers couldn't preach 'bout de Gospel an' God. Dey didn' 'low him to. All he could preach 'bout was obey. Obey de marster, obey de overseer, obey dis, an' obey dat." However, what they did hear preached about Christ, created a desire to seek Him in secret. Mr. Mathews continues saying, "Sometimes dey sneak off an' meet in one of de other cabins at night. Den each one bring a pot an' dey put dere head in de pot to keep de echoes from getting back an' somebody hearing dem. Den dey pray in de pot." (Federal Writer's Project, United States Work Project Administration, "Born in Slavery: Slave Narratives from the Federal Writers' Project, 1936-1938, Texas Narratives," vol. 16, part 3, William Mathews, p. 69. http://memory.loc.gov/cgi-bin/ampage? [accessed June 16, 2004]).

3. "Slave Narratives: Laura Thornton," MyFamily.com.

4. Federal Writer's Project, United States Work Project Administration, "Born in Slavery: Slave Narratives from the Federal Writers' Project, 1936-1938, North Carolina Narratives," vol. 11, part 2, Alex Woods, p. 416. http://memory.loc.gov/cgi-bin/ampage?collId=mesn&fileName=112/mesn112.db&recNum=417 (accessed June 4, 2004).

5. Federal Writer's Project, United States Work Project Administration, "Born in Slavery: Slave Narratives from the Federal Writers' Project, 1936-1938, Arkansas Narratives," vol. 2, part 1, Lucretia Alexander, p. 35. http://memory.loc.gov/cgi-bin/ampage?collId=mesn&fileName=021/mesn021.db&recNum=36 (accessed June 4, 2004).

6. Federal Writer's Project, United States Work Project Administration, "Born in Slavery: Slave Narratives from the Federal Writers' Project, 1936-1938, North Carolina Narratives," vol. 11, part 1, Kitty Hill, p. 425. http://memory.loc.gov/cgi-bin/ampage?collId=mesn&fileName=111/mesn111.db&recNum=425 (accessed June 4 2004).

7. Raboteau, *Slave Religion: The Invisible Institution in the Antebellum South* (New York: Oxford University Press, 1978), p. 216.

8. "Slave Narratives: Edd Roby," MyFamily.com. Research for slave narratives was gathered from several resources. The collection contains over 20,000 pages of type-scripted interviews with more than 3,500 former slaves, collected over a 10-year period, from 1929-1939. Much of this information is with the Library of Congress. Of course, there are a few references to slaves who had other religious beliefs and folk practices on plantations (Muslims, conjuring, superstitions and folk religions). More outstandingly, there are more than 300 descriptions from Christian slaves having secret prayer meetings, and half of them mentioned using kettles, cooking pots, wash pots, barrels and other means to muffle their voices to pray for freedom. Many accounts also include digging holes in the ground to pray, sometimes in conjunction with these vessels. Once in the hole, they put

the pot or barrel on top to cover them as they prayed, preventing them from being heard. Ellen Butler, ex-slave recalls, "Dey hab big holes out in de fiel's dey git down in and pray. Dey done dat way 'cause de w'ite folks didn' want 'em to pray. Dey uster pray for freedom." Instead of being used ritually, these methods were used practically to conceal their prayer times for fear of being caught and punished. Of this she says, "I dunno how they l'arn to pray. . . . I reckon de Lawd jis mek 'em know how to pray." (Federal Writer's Project, United States Work Project Administration, "Born in Slavery: Slave Narratives from the Federal Writers' Project, 1936-1938, Texas Narratives," vol. 16, part 1, Ex-Slave Stories, Texas, Ellen Butler, p. 177. http://memory.loc.gov/cgi-bin/ampage?collId=mesn&file Name=161/mesn161" [accessed June 16, 2004]). Like my ancestors, James Southall (interviewed November 5, 1937, in Oklahoma), was part of this Christian remnant of slaves. Mr. Southall, a licensed Baptist minister, remembered praying "in holes" and "praying under cooking pots" to deaden the sound as he prayed. When asked if he believed in other plantation folk religions, he says, "I learned a long time ago dat dey was nothing to charms. How could a rabbit's foot bring me good luck? De Bible teaches me better'n dat. . . . I believe in praying fer what we want and need." (Federal Writer's Project, United States Work Project Administration, "Born in Slavery: Slave Narratives from the Federal Writers' Project, 1936-1938, Oklahoma Narratives," vol. 13, James Southall, p. 306. http://memory.loc.gov/cgi-bin/ampage?collId=mesn& fileName=130/mesn130.db&recNum=312&itemLink=D [accessed June 16, 2004]). James Southall and my ancestors were not alone, as evidenced by the others cited in this chapter. Hebrews 11:38 says these were people of "whom the world was not worthy," who dwelt in "holes in the ground," (and also under cooking pots I add), praying for you and me.

9. Ibid.

10. Federal Writer's Project, United States Work Project Administration, "Born in Slavery: Slave Narratives from the Federal Writers' Project, 1936-1938, Indiana Narratives," vol. 5, Candus Richardson, pp. 158-159. http://memory.loc.gov/cgi-bin/ampage?collId=mesn&fileName=050/ mesn050.db&recNum=162 (accessed June 4, 2004).

11. Ibid.

12. James Washington, *Conversations with God: Two Centuries of Prayers by African Americans* (New York: HarperCollins Publishers, 1994), p. 51.

13. Ibid., p. 46.

14. Federal Writer's Project, United States Work Project Administration, "Born in Slavery: Slave Narratives from the Federal Writers' Project, 1936-1938, Arkansas Narratives," vol. 2, part 6, Tom Robinson, p. 64. http://memory.loc.gov/cgi-bin/query/r?ammem/mesnbib:@field

(DOCID+@lit(mesn/026/066061)) (accessed June 4, 2004).

15. Harriet Beecher Stowe, *Key to Uncle Tom's Cabin* (New York: Signet Classics, 1966), p. 227.

16. Taken from sermon notes, February 14, 1998, Dutch Sheets, Dallas, TX.

17. Dutch Sheets, *Praying For America* (Ventura, CA: Regal Books, 2001), p. 22.

18. Peter Marshall and David Manuel, *Sounding Forth the Trumpet* (Grand Rapids, MI: Fleming H. Revell, 1999), p. 16.

19. George W. Bush, "Remarks by the President on Goree Island" (speech, Goree Island, Senegal, July 8, 2003), *White House*. http://www.white house.gov/news/releases/2003/07/20030708-1.html (accessed June 8, 2004).

20. See 1 Peter 2:9; Hebrews 11:36-40; Revelation 8:3-7.

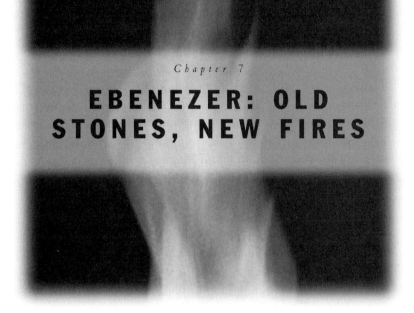

Chapter 7

EBENEZER: OLD STONES, NEW FIRES

Then Elijah said to all the people, "Come near to me." So all the people
came near to him. And he repaired the altar of the LORD which had
been torn down. Elijah took twelve stones according to the number of
the tribes of the sons of Jacob, to whom the word of the LORD had come,
saying, "Israel shall be your name."

1 KINGS 18:30-31

The building of altars for our lives is another truth seen in the
place of intercession. In Old Testament times, altars were built
not only as places of sacrifice but also as memorials for marking
and remembering significant events. Abraham built an altar to
the Lord at Shechem, where God first promised him the land of
Canaan: "The LORD appeared to Abram and said, 'To your
descendants I will give this land.' So he built an altar there to the

LORD who had appeared to him" (Gen. 12:7).

The prophet Samuel built a memorial near the town of Mizpah to mark a victory that the Lord had given Israel over the Philistines. He named it Ebenezer, meaning "the stone of help" and stated, "Thus far the LORD has helped us" (1 Sam. 7.12). How does this altar building relate to us today? Are we supposed to build literal altars or memorials? That, of course, isn't necessary. Yet we do build them in our hearts.

ALTARS AND MEMORIALS

In *Intercessory Prayer*, I (Dutch) tell the story of a young girl who had been in a comatose state for two and a half years. Her brain had basically been destroyed, eaten up by infection caused by viral encephalitis. After a year of intense and persistent intercession, to the amazement of the medical world, the Lord restored her to complete health. After spending 60 to 70 hours (during a one-year period) praying over her lifeless body, I will never forget the day that I saw her awake and alert—and I built a memorial there. I also built a family memorial when my wife, Ceci, was healed by God of an ovarian cyst. There are many other memorials that stand as monuments to the faithfulness of God in my life. Today, when nagging doubts try to trouble my mind in order to convince me that God will not come through for me in a particular situation, I revisit my Ebenezer. I whisper quietly, "Thus far He has helped me."

Altars and memorials are not merely personal; they are also objects and meeting places where God remembers His friends. They are used to connect the generations. For example, when the Lord parted the Jordan, God told Joshua to get memorial stones, which were used to build altars, so that ensuing generations would be introduced to His faithfulness (see Josh. 4:8-9,21).

God doesn't care that much about land, artifacts, relics or piles of stone. What He loves is the people they represent—people who have moved His heart. When the Lord saw the 12 memorial stones of Joshua's day, He didn't see a mound of rocks. He saw 12 great-great-grandsons of His covenant friend Abraham, who had left all to follow Him. When He sees Will's cast-iron kettle, He doesn't see a 200-year-old pot; instead, He sees people of all races who fellowshiped with His Son in laying down their lives to intercede for others. Today, we use this kettle as a memorial stone to rebuild the altars of revival.

Abraham's grandson Jacob had this understanding: "So Jacob rose early in the morning, and took the stone that he had put under his head and set it up as a pillar and poured oil on its top" (Gen. 28:18). The word "pillar" could be translated "memorial stone" or "monument." We do much the same today in building memorials at significant battle sites or in memory of great leaders.

The kettle reminds us of the living stones, the pillars of faith, who have laid a foundation for revival. It calls to mind the sacrifice of others on Christ's behalf for this nation. An Ebenezer, the kettle reminds us of how God has helped us with spiritual awakenings that have revived America and ended slavery.

THE REVIVALISTS

In this chapter, we talk about revivalists whom God used during the first and second Great Awakenings. If you've studied revival before, some of these revivalists (the Wesley brothers, Whitefield, etc.) may be familiar to you, but others won't be—particularly the African Americans.

There were many great African-American revivalists and abolitionists. It would take many books to write about Frederick Douglass, Absalom Jones and others. In fact, entire volumes could be written about the few men and women we mention in this chapter.

What we desire to do is show the heart of a few well-known revivalists and their little-known stance against slavery, as well as highlight significant African-American men and women rarely mentioned in revival history. You will see a remnant of black and white people operating as the True Church, and you will come to understand the impact they had on society. More than your getting just another history lesson, we want you to connect with the passion and abandonment these great men and women of faith possessed. As you visit the Ebenezers, the stories they built will fuel your faith for awakening today.

Revivalists Against Slavery

America was set on fire by the flame that burned within John Wesley, Charles Wesley and George Whitefield. The Wesleys and Whitefield preached to thousands, saw massive conversions and were very vocal in their stand against slavery during the first Great Awakening. When it was frequently asked, "Does the Negro have a soul?" Whitefield was the first to give the positive reply that there was no difference between the soul of a white man and the soul of a black man.

Regarding slavery, Whitefield sent a scathing letter that was published in newspapers throughout the 13 colonies:

> Your dogs are caroused and fondled at your tables, but your slaves, who are frequently styled dogs or beasts, have no equal privilege. . . . "Go to, ye rich men, weep and howl, for your miseries shall come upon you!"

Behold the provision of the poor Negroes, which have reaped your fields, which is by you denied them, crieth, and the cries of them which have reaped have come into the ears of the Lord of Sabaoth![1]

Many kingdoms were being upset during this time. The religious and social systems of the day were shaken. Whitefield, Gilbert Tennant and other revivalists noted with satisfaction the presence of black people swelling the crowds who flocked to hear their powerful message of salvation. Whitefield recounted an occasion in Philadelphia, Pennsylvania, in 1740 when nearly 50 blacks offered him thanks for what God had done in their lives.[2]

Again and again Edwards was heard to say, "O Lord, give me New England! O Lord, give me New England!"

Jonathan Edwards

Jonathan Edwards became the most noteworthy of the evangelists during the first Great Awakening. God used Edwards greatly in advancing the revival from 1740 to 1746. Edwards became distraught and very concerned over the souls of New England. He fasted for three days without food, water or sleep, praying for New England.

Again and again Edwards was heard to say, "O Lord, give me New England! O Lord, give me New England!" This three-day pursuit of God's presence was as far reaching as that of any other time in his life. In *The Power of Prayer and Fasting*, Ronnie Floyd gives this account:

Lathered in sweat and tears, when Jonathan Edwards rose from his knees and made his way into the pulpit that historic Sunday, those who saw him were transfixed, saying later that he looked as though he had been gazing straight into the face of God. Three days of fasting and praying had prepared his heart to preach the sermon of his life. Even before he began to speak, said eyewitnesses, spiritual dread and the heaviness of a conviction of sin fell upon his audience. And then he spoke his message, "Sinners in the Hands of an Angry God." He held his sermon notes so close that the audience could not see his face. He preached and preached until people in that crowded assembly were moved almost beyond control. It's said that one man jumped up and rushed down the aisle crying, "Mr. Edwards, have mercy!" Others clutched the backs of the pews for fear of falling into the fiery pit of hell itself. Most thought the Day of Judgment had dawned. And for some, undoubtedly it had. Everyone in that assembly found himself standing in awe of the holiness of God.[3]

Jonathan Edwards affirmed God's presence and power as a reality. Edwards reported:

The affection was quickly propagated throughout the room; many of the young people and children . . . appeared to be overcome with a sense of the greatness and glory of divine things, and with admiration, love, joy and praise and compassion to others that looked upon themselves as in a state of nature (unsaved); and many others at the same time were overcome with distress about their sinful and miserable condition; so that the whole room was full of nothing but outcries, faintings, convulsions, and the like. It was pretty often so, that there were some that were so affected, and their bodies so overcome, that they could not go home, but were obliged to stay all night where they were.[4]

What an Ebenezer! God's heart was the foundation; Edwards's passion and devotion, the mortar; and the souls of men were the stones as this great preacher helped erect an Ebenezer we still remember today, the first Great Awakening.

It was said that the presence of God was so powerful that Northampton, Massachusetts, was under the very cloud of God. Even miles away from a church service, people would fall down in the streets, convicted of their sins. We, along with many of our friends, prayed at this historic location on the Kettle Tour, asking God for the old stones and the new fire!

Although he was known for his sermon previously mentioned, the majority of Edwards's revelation and teaching were on the love of God. "Sinners in the Hands of an Angry God" was preached to an apostate, lukewarm church, not necessarily to the lost. Edwards's teachings on God's grace and love are still considered to be some of the best expositions on those subjects today. Many feel that it was these sermons that brought slaves into what is called New Light preaching.[5]

Edwards noted:

There are several Negroes who, from what was seen in them and what is discernible in them since, appear to have been truly born again in the late remarkable season.[6]

The Conversion of Slaves

The Holy Spirit also influenced slaves in a very deep and profound way. Many reported that although they could not read (it was against the law), they were saved through trances, visions and angelic visitations. These slaves then became carriers of revival. Here's one example:

> One day while in the field plowing I heard a voice. . . .
> I looked but saw no one. . . . Everything got dark, and
> I was unable to stand any longer. . . . With this I
> began to cry, Mercy! Mercy! Mercy! As I prayed an
> angel came and touched me, and I looked new . . .
> and there came a soft voice saying, "My little one, I have
> loved you with an everlasting love. You are a chosen
> vessel unto the Lord." . . . I must have been in this
> trance more than an hour. I went on to the barn and
> found my master waiting for me. . . . I began to tell
> him of my experiences. . . . My master sat watching
> and listening to me, and then he began to cry. He
> turned from me and said in a broken voice, "Morte, I
> believe you are a preacher. From now on you can preach
> to the people here on my place. . . . But tomorrow
> morning, Sunday, I want you to preach to my family
> and my neighbors". . . . The next morning at the time
> appointed I stood up on two planks in front of the
> porch of the big house and, without a Bible or any-
> thing, I began to preach to my master and the people.
> My thoughts came so fast that I could hardly speak fast
> enough. My soul caught on fire, and soon I had them
> all in tears. . . . I told them that they must be born
> again and that their souls must be freed from the
> shackles of hell.[7]

God still remembers this friend of His. He is just waiting for someone to "visit" the memorial that no doubt has been erected in the Spirit and to stay there in prayer until yesterday empowers today.

A Lasting Impact

Long after the first Great Awakening, both free blacks and slaves were still affected by these revivals.

> "Uncle" Jack, an African-born slave and a Baptist convert, preached in Nottoway County, Virginia, in 1792. Jack impressed some white church members enough to make them purchase his freedom and settle him on a farm. Jack continued to preach for forty years and had the satisfaction of converting his former master's son.[8]

Toward the end of the eighteenth century, the Methodists licensed Henry Evans, an African-American free man and a shoemaker by trade, as a local preacher. Evans was responsible for "the planting of Methodism" in Fayetteville, North Carolina. Originally preaching to black people only, he attracted the attention of some prominent whites, and, ironically, the number of whites who came to hear him preach soon outnumbered and supplanted the blacks.[9] Evans was eventually displaced by a white minister, but he continued to serve as an assistant in the church he founded until his death in 1810.

In 1792, the people of a Portsmouth, Virginia, congregation lost their pastor and "employed Josiah (or Jacob) Bishop, a black man of considerable talents, to preach for them. They thought so much of him that they paid for his freedom and his entire family as well."[10] A slave named Simon was set free by a white congregation to exercise his gifts in Roanoke, Virginia, because "they thought him ordained by God to preach the gospel."[11]

Francis Asbury

Francis Asbury was a key figure in the spread of the gospel in America. On the Kettle Tour we visited one of his "wells" in Philadelphia— Saint George Methodist Church— and drank deeply from its rich heritage. Asbury established circuit preaching for the Methodists. Circuit preachers traveled over rough terrain all over America, braving perils from men, wild animals and disease. Asbury had a recorded 672 circuit riders. The circuit preachers preached on the themes of free grace, instant salvation and sanctification through the infilling of the Holy Spirit. Wesley Duewel sheds more light on Asbury: "When Asbury arrived in America, there were 1,160 Methodists. When he died, there were 214,235. He ordained more than 3,000 ministers and preached more than 17,000 sermons."[12] Asbury was so loved by America that when he died, half the town of Baltimore (25,000 people) marched in his funeral procession. What a memorial! Somebody, please, visit it!

Asbury and Hosier were eighteenth-century Cape Hatteras lighthouses, black and white voices spiraling together, pointing the way to God's harbor of salvation: Jesus Christ.

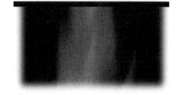

Asbury, a disciple of Wesley, took a hard stand against slavery. He even spoke with George Washington and urged him to sign a document that would emancipate slaves. Francis Asbury believed in the synergy of the races. He traveled with an African-American preacher named Harry Hosier. The two rode on horseback across the country and preached together. Asbury and Hosier traveled as co-laborers in Christ. Hosier wasn't Asbury's slave, servant or helper; he was his brother. They were eighteenth-century Cape Hatteras lighthouses, black and white voices spiraling together, pointing the way to God's safety from the storm, His harbor of salvation: Jesus Christ.

Hosier, who could not read or write, was known as an awesome prayer warrior who later became a preacher. Born into slavery in North Carolina, he was freed from his Maryland master shortly after the Revolutionary War. His sermon "The Barren Fig Tree" preached at Adam's Chapel in Fairfax County, Virginia, in May 1781, was the first recorded Methodist sermon by an African American. Hosier eventually became a more popular speaker than Asbury—much to the delight of Asbury! Hosier preached in the historic Saint George Methodist Church in Philadelphia, Pennsylvania, and ministered in white and black congregations—indeed, he was admired equally among people of both races. His travels took him up and down the Atlantic seaboard. Harry Hosier is heralded by Methodists as one of the greatest preachers of his time. They credit his influence as one of the most important factors in the early spread of the Methodist church in America. Besides traveling with Asbury, Hosier also traveled with other white ministers, including Freeborn Garretson.[13]

Garretson grew up in a family that owned slaves. During the Great Awakening, he was born again, and God broke his heart over slavery in America. Garretson went into his family prayer meeting one day and told everyone that freedom in Christ means freedom for everyone; therefore, all of the slaves whom he had just inherited were now free. Ebenezer!

After releasing all of his slaves, Garretson became a traveling Methodist preacher. His travels took him to Delaware, where slave Richard Allen was preaching the gospel. Allen was a fiery preacher, and many were converted in the neighborhoods where he spoke. Garretson was invited to speak on the plantation where Allen was a slave, and Allen's slave master was converted. Just as Garretson had done, Allen's slave master also set all of his slaves free. Ebenezer times two! Richard Allen and Freeborn Garretson became traveling altar builders preaching together in many places, including Asbury's Saint George Methodist Church.

Eventually, blacks and whites had services together in Baptist and Methodist churches. Often blacks outnumbered whites. Congregations had to split for convenience and growth reasons. But not all church splits were cordial. African-American Richard Allen started Bethel Church after blacks at the Saint George Methodist Church in Philadelphia had been offended during a prayer meeting. Not everyone in the church shared Asbury's heart. At first, white church officials had said that they would not acknowledge the blacks. Allen had replied: "If you deny us your name, you cannot seal up the Scriptures from us, and deny us a name in Heaven. We believe heaven is open to all who worship in spirit and truth."[14] Bethel Church was started in 1794. It drew attention from the slaveholding Southerners and from people up and down the East Coast. In 1816, Allen formed a denomination called the African Methodist Episcopal Church. Allen was a powerful speaker and preacher, and later he became a legislator in government. For those who care to dig, there is an altar worth rebuilding.

THE DEBATE ON SLAVERY

George Mason was one of the wealthiest men in America. He owned 15,000 acres in Virginia and 85,000 acres in Ohio. Even though he was one of the largest plantation owners in Virginia, he was opposed to slavery. He was a state delegate, a lawyer, a judge, a political philosopher and a planter. On August 22, 1787, he made this statement at the Constitutional Convention during the debate on slavery, and this statement later proved to be prophetic:

> Every master of slaves is born a petty tyrant. They [slave owners] bring the judgment of heaven upon a country. As nations cannot be rewarded or punished in the next world, they must be in this. By an inevitable chain of causes and effects, Providence punishes national sins, by national calamities.[15]

Although many changes happened in New England and slavery was ended in the North because of revival, new Southern states entering the Union didn't want to divest of their slaves. The revival that had prepared the way for their freedom from the oppression of England had not done enough to change their view of slavery in America.

With the application of Missouri for admission to statehood in 1820, the slavery issue again erupted. So great was the storm of the controversy over whether it would come in as a slave or free state, that Southern members of the United States House of Representatives and United States Senate actually expressed the possibility of their states' leaving the union.[16]

William Wilberforce

Another of Wesley's disciples was William Wilberforce. At first, Wilberforce thought he would go into the clergy, but he was led to go into politics instead. God needs altar builders in every area of life. With the passion and support of his spiritual father,

Wilberforce used the power of God to change society in England and end slavery there. Wilberforce was greatly influenced by Wesley, who was then 88 and close to dying. Wesley's last written communication was to Wilberforce:

> Unless God has raised you up for this very thing, you will be worn out by the opposition of men and devils, but if God be for you who can be against you? Are all of them together stronger than God? Oh, be not weary of well doing. Go on in the name of God, and in the power of His might, till even American slavery, the vilest that ever saw the sun, shall vanish away before it. That He that has guided you from your youth may continue to strengthen you in this and all things, is the prayer of, Dear Sir, Your affectionate servant, John Wesley.[17]

A few days after writing this letter, Wesley died, giving to Wilberforce his mantle for revival that would end slavery in England. Slavery was ended in Britain by 1833, and that began to stir the debate about slavery in the southern part of America.

Charles Finney

One of the most powerful preachers during the Second Great Awakening was Charles Finney. He left us some wonderful Ebenezers. Whole regions would come under the convicting work of the Holy Spirit, and people miles away would be touched by the manifest presence of God. It is recorded that Finney's revivals had such an impact on Rochester, New York, that there was no crime in that city for five years. Incredible stories have been told about how God used Finney to bring revival, social justice and transformation.

Finney also took a strong stand against slavery, calling it sin.

He preached hard against the injustice. Toward the end of his life, he pastored a church that began to grow rapidly, and so he began a building program. When asked if the new church would need a balcony where blacks could sit, Finney said that there would be no need for a balcony. He said that everyone would sit on the same level, because everyone is on the same level in Christ. When the townspeople found out about this, they burned down the church—the fire department even refused to put out the flames. The congregation itself put out the fire and successfully rebuilt the church.[18]

Theodore Weld

Theodore Weld, a white minister, was converted in one of

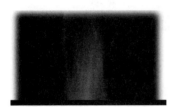

Finney's meetings in Oberlin, Ohio. After his conversion experience, Weld became a disciple of Finney's and a traveling evangelist who saw many souls come to Christ. He took a strong stand for temperance and later against slavery. Eventually, Weld used his revival anointing to become one of the foremost voices against slavery.

Slave owners came to Theodore Weld's meetings to refute his claims, but they would become convicted, return to their plantations and release their slaves.

Weld was powerfully used of God. With bold humility, he would speak in graphic detail to describe what slaves had to endure, and he had slaves tell their stories. The presence of God flooded his meetings, and his audience was often reduced to tears. Slave owners came to his meetings to refute his claims, but they would

become convicted, return to their plantations and release their slaves. One slave owner, James Birney, became an outspoken abolitionist. Wealthy men such as Arthur Tappan and his brother, Lewis, became Christian abolitionists and funded the cause. Whole cities and regions switched from slavery to abolition.[19]

However, Weld wasn't without opposition. He was called the most mobbed man in America. His altar building, like the apostle Paul's, stirred up much demonic opposition. People threw vegetables, rocks and bottles at him as he spoke. He would stand for hours and wait out boisterous crowds.

Weld's worst mobbing occurred when he was headed for Troy, Ohio. Knowing that Troy was full of opposition, he decided to start at a city adjacent to Troy and work his way in. But an angry mob from Troy came to where Weld was and beat him badly. This mobbing proved to be fatal to his voice—afterward he could only speak slightly above a whisper. His voice grew weaker, and eventually he lost it completely, but not before he went to Troy and spoke. Weld held a series of meetings there, and by the time he had finished, the town had converted to abolition. The entire state of Ohio was changed from slavery to abolition because of Theodore Weld.[20] Someone needs to drink from this well of revival, and rebuild the memorial.

Harriet Beecher Stowe

One of the people whom Weld had a great influence on was a girl whose father, Lyman Beecher, was the president of the school that Weld had attended. After attending Weld's meetings and reading his book *Slavery As It Is in America*, this girl heeded her sister's advice and began to write a novel based on historical facts. The book opened the eyes of Americans and people around the world to the atrocity of slavery from the Christian perspective of revivalists. Even the location of her home had helped prepare her for this assignment.

Although Stowe didn't realize it, she lived across the street from a house in Cincinnati, Ohio, that was part of the Underground Railroad. Escaped slaves from the South would tell her about the condition of slavery. She gathered this information and used these facts, but with fictional names, to reveal the true nature of slavery. Stowe had a vision while in church and "ran home to begin the novel that was unstoppable to her, burning her up like the zeal of God's house."[21] The Holy Spirit would seize her, and she would write profusely. God breathed on this work, and it was a worldwide best-seller. It was the first Christian book to impact society the way that it did. The name of the book? *Uncle Tom's Cabin.*

Released in 1850, the book enjoyed a phenomenal circulation, especially considering the fact that people in the 1850s didn't have the printing presses that we do today. The first week of its release, *Uncle Tom's Cabin* sold more than 10,000 copies. In one year, 300,000 copies were sold in America, and more than 1 million bootlegged copies were estimated to have been sold in Europe. *Uncle Tom's Cabin* had a profound influence around the world. For example, in Berlin, Germany, over one of the tunnels, the words "Uncle Tom's Cabin" are written in German. It is said that when Abraham Lincoln met Stowe, he said, "So this is the little woman, who began the big war."[22] And built a big monument!

Amanda Smith

Another woman used powerfully during this period but known by few is Amanda Smith. She was born in slavery, and God delivered her from slavery through the prayers of her grandmother.

Amanda Smith had a powerful prayer life as a toddler, but she didn't come of faith until she was a teenager. After evangelist Phoebe Palmer prayed for her to receive the baptism of the

Holy Spirit, she began to walk in a nearness to God that she hadn't previously known.

Smith had an open vision in which she saw the word "go" written in fire over her head. She knew that this was God calling her to the mission field and that God was telling her to go into all the world and preach the gospel. Although this was during the time of slavery, Amanda ministered in mostly Caucasian congregations and traveled around the world preaching the gospel. This was an incredible accomplishment for a woman, especially an African-American woman during the time of slavery in the mid-1800s.

Smith walked in an incredible anointing and ministered with signs and wonders following. She preached in a womanly and very sophisticated manner but with great passion and conviction. She taught on the love of God, holiness and the power of the Holy Spirit. Smith was known for her incredible life of prayer and fasting. Once, while in India, she was pursued by an angry mob. As she knelt in prayer, the approaching mob, which had previously attacked other missionaries, stopped jeering and threatening as she prayed. The glory of God could be seen on her, and everyone around her stopped in awe. By the time she had finished praying, the mob had turned docile. She stood and preached the gospel to all present, including those in the mob. Amanda built an Ebenezer that someone needs to visit.

The Civil War

Revival did move through the South, but slaveholders didn't want to give up their idolatry to mammon and the resulting slavery. The inevitable happened, and the Civil War came. Even during the Civil War, revival continued. It is reported that church services were held in the evenings, and soldiers from the North and the South would have services together. In the mornings, they would get up and start the fight again. Most people thought the South would win, but they forgot about the praying remnant of slaves and abolitionists.

On September 22, 1862, President Abraham Lincoln issued the Emancipation Proclamation, which began the process to end slavery in America. The Battle of Gettysburg was the turning point, and from that point on, the North gained momentum and won the war.

> Had enough hearts been touched by it [revival], the Civil War could have been avoided. As it was, instead of delivering America from her horrendous ordeal, it prepared her to endure and survive it.[23]

England and New England were shaken when the first Great Awakening happened. That which may have been God's offer of a divine remedy—revival—became divine preparation for the colonists' war for freedom—the Revolutionary War. Colonial America was set free from the British, while the institution of slavery stayed intact. Nevertheless, it was God's intention that everyone be free. The Body of Christ kept praying, and then the coals, fire and lightning of Revelation 8:5 were again poured out. America was rocked by the Second Great Awakening, as God tipped the bowls of prayer over this nation once more. And as before, that which could have been the divine remedy—revival— prepared a nation for divine judgment—the Civil War.

Finally, the institution that everyone thought would always stay intact was abolished. Cries in bondage had come up before God's throne as incense; and just as He did for Israel in Egypt, He tipped the bowl of deliverance and parted the waters of slavery. He remembered the cries of slaves around kettles, circuit-riding lighthouses and reformers like Wesley and Wilberforce.

Transforming their lives into living stones of remembrance, He stacked them one upon another and built a lasting memorial called Freedom.

THE RAIN OF REVIVAL

My (Will's) family has been left a kettle as a memorial stone. It connects us with living stones who have preceded us, in the same way that the stones of Joshua's day did. It is not an idol; rather, it simply connects us with the history of what Christ, who is the same yesterday, today and forever, did in their time. It is God's way of saying, "The same revival power that was available to them is present for you today." Connect with the God of our fathers!

When Elijah had his showdown with Baal, he gathered 12 stones to build an altar (see 1 Kings 18:31). They were actually stones from an old altar that had fallen down. As he did this, Elijah was reminding God that he remembered His faithfulness to his forefathers when they crossed the Jordan. He was asking God to restore the Israelites to their first love and first works. Like Elijah, we must gather old stones, the memories of His faithfulness to our forefathers, for a new fire in the Church that will revive the nation again.

Today, in much the same way, we can use the memories of God's past faithfulness as stones to rebuild the altars of revival in America. Just as Elijah remembered the God of his past, and revival came into his present and future, we must lay hold of the memories of what God has done with past pillars of faith and ask Him to send new fire to America. We have an altar in front of us that lies in ruins, and God is asking us to rebuild it.

After the fire fell on Elijah's altar and the people cried out to the God of Israel, the three-year-long drought ended, and rain came to Israel. This, however, was not without Elijah's contending for it in prayer (see 1 Kings 18:41-45). Elijah prayed fervently until he saw a cloud the size of a man's hand. It grew into storm clouds and released God's restorative rain.

There is another cloud the size of a man's hand over America today. But who will ascend the hill of the Lord one more time and travail in prayer until revival showers are poured out over our nation again? Elijah was persistent. As he prayed for rain, Elijah sent his servant back seven times to look out over the sea. We must look beyond the sea of sin that has piled up in this nation and contend with eyes of faith for mercy to come over our horizon. Take another look. Let's not despise small beginnings, but let's keep crying out until the cloud increases and God releases His rain of revival. It's not too late to heal our past and write the history God wants for America.

O, holy church universal, throughout all countries and nations! O ye great cloud of witnesses, of all people and languages and tongues! Differing in many doctrines, but united in crying, "Worthy is the Lamb that was slain, for he hath redeemed us from all iniquity!"—awake!—arise up!—be not silent! Testify against this heresy of the latter day, which, if it were possible, is deceiving the very elect. Your God, your glory, is slandered. Answer with the voice of many waters and mighty thunderings! Answer with the innumerable multitude in heaven, who cry, day and night, "Holy, holy, holy! Just and true are thy ways, O king of saints!"[24]

(Prayer of Harriet Beecher Stowe.)

Notes

1. Arnold Dallimore, *George Whitefield* (Wheaton, IL: Crossway Books, 1990), p. 79.
2. Albert J. Raboteau, *Slave Religion* (New York: Oxford University Press, 1978), p. 128.
3. Ronnie Floyd, *The Power of Prayer and Fasting* (Nashville, TN: Broadman and Holman Publishers, 1997), p. 100.
4. Ron Phillips, *Awakened by the Spirit* (Nashville, TN: Thomas Nelson Publishers, 1999), p. 104.
5. New Light sermons focused on the love and grace of God. Preachers often joined Old Testament subjects of freedom from oppression with Jesus' teaching of God's loving everyone equally, a message which appealed to slaves. Edwards, Wesley and Whitefield preached this message, stressing the need for everyone to experience a rebirth in Jesus. These eye-opening New Light sermons are one reason the period was called the Great Awakening.
6. Raboteau, *Slave Religion*, p. 128.
7. Bruno Chenu, *The Trouble I've Seen: The Big Book of Negro Spirituals* (Valley Forge, PA: Judson Press, 2003), pp. 53-55.
8. Raboteau, *Slave Religion*, p. 135.
9. Ibid.
10. Ibid., p. 134.
11. Ibid., p. 135.
12. Wesley Duewel, *Heroes of the Holy Life* (Grand Rapids, MI: Zondervan Publishing House, 2002), p. 21.
13. "Harry Hosier, The General Commission on Archives and History," *The United Methodist Church*. http://www.gcah.org/Methodlist_Bio/Harry_Hosier.htm (accessed October 30, 2003).
14. Richard Allen, quoted in Quinton Dixie and Juan Williams, *This Far by Faith* (New York: HarperCollins Publishers, 2003), p. 20.
15. William Federer, *America's God and Country Encyclopedia of Quotations* (Coppell, TX: Fame Publishing, 1994), p. 423.
16. Peter Marshall and David Manuel, *Sounding Forth the Trumpet* (Grand Rapids, MI: Fleming H. Revell, 1997), p. 15.
17. John Wesley, quoted in Lon Fendall, *William Wilberforce: Abolitionist, Politician, Writer* (Uhrichville, OH: Barbour Books, 2002), p. 88.
18. Charles G. Finney, *Revival Lectures* (Grand Rapids, MI: Fleming H. Revell, 1993), p. 325.
19. Marshall and Manuel, *Sounding Forth the Trumpet*, pp. 31-38.
20. Ibid.
21. Source unknown.
22. Harriet Beecher Stowe, *Keys to Uncle Tom's Cabin* (New York: Signet Classic, 1966), n.p.

23. Marshall and Manuel, *Sounding Forth the Trumpet*, p. 12.
24. Stowe, *Keys to Uncle Tom's Cabin*, p. 223.

Chapter 8

THE JOSIAH AWAKENING

*Josiah was eight years old when he became king, and he reigned
thirty-one years in Jerusalem; and his mother's name was Jedidah
the daughter of Adaiah of Bozkath. He did right in the sight of the
LORD and walked in all the way of his father David, nor did
he turn aside to the right or to the left.*

2 KINGS 22:1-2

Will and I, along with our team, took the kettle to Plymouth,
Massachusetts, where the Pilgrims had come ashore, and we
prayed, "Lord, *remember* the covenant our forefathers made with
you here." We took the kettle to Jamestown and, at the site of the
first church in America, asked God to "*remember* the prayers
offered here and raise up the righteous foundations that were
established in this place."

We carried the kettle to the site of one of the first *black* churches in America, founded by Moses and Gowan Pamphlet in Williamsburg.[1] At the site of this brush harbor church, there is no building there now, but we laid in the grass under the kettle and asked God to *remember* our righteous forefathers. We rededicated ourselves to their dream of equality and asked for the synergy of the ages to occur—for God to *remember* their commitment and dedication and to allow us to drink from their well.

We prayed around the kettle at Gettysburg, asking God to *remember* the blood that had been shed there for a righteous and noble cause. "As You have before for this nation, in Your wrath *remember* mercy," we pleaded.

We knelt around the kettle at Howard University—one of the historic black universities in America—and we prayed that black Americans would come into the fullness of their destiny in this land. We asked God to *remember* the dreams of Howard Thurman, Martin Luther King, Jr., and other African-American leaders.

We visited Williams College, the birthplace of missions in America through the Haystack Revival; Yale University, where Timothy Dwight led a revival in 1802 and a third of the student body was converted; St. George's Methodist Church, from which Francis Asbury sent circuit riders like Peter Cartwright around the nation carrying revival fire; the church in Northampton, Massachusetts, where Jonathan Edwards preached. In each of these places and many more, we prayed, "Please, Lord, *remember.*" There are no words to describe how holy and powerful these times were.

REMEMBRANCES

One of the biggest crazes going on in America is scrapbook making. It has taken shape as a legitimate market within the field of arts and crafts. The reason it is seeing such momentum is that God put within us the ability and propensity to *remember*. We are made in the likeness of the greatest maker and recorder of memories, God Himself. Malachi 3:16 says that He honors those who honor Him by recording their stories in a book of remembrance. On the Kettle Tour we reminded God of His precious scrapbook material. We also gave Him some memories of our own.

Memories are powerful. As we read the Bible, the Lord is basically sharing with us His scrapbook—the memories of those who have moved His heart and shaped history with Him. Connecting with these individuals who have shaped history with God, whether they are Bible patriarchs or heroes of faith centuries later, makes something come alive within us.

For me (Will), something powerful happened when I connected with the people who prayed underneath my family's 200-year-old kettle. The history of God's faithfulness to our family has forever changed me.

THE JOSIAH AWAKENING

Through a dream the Lord gave me, I began to understand how important passing down history is to Him. In the dream, I was becoming the steward of an 8-year-old boy who had a bad family background. When I asked if he wanted me to take him in, he said, "Yes. I had a vision of this related to 222." Unlike other dreams, when I awoke I immediately knew the interpretation. The 222 was 2 Kings 22, where the story of the 8-year-old king Josiah takes place. Josiah had a bad family background: His father, grandfather and others before him had been wicked kings.

But Hilkiah the priest found the book of the law, which contained Israel's history. Josiah's life was changed as he read this book. He was touched and moved by God's past faithfulness, and it appears that when Josiah read about God's history with David and Israel, something inside him came alive. We're told, "He did right in the sight of the LORD and walked in all the way of his father David" (2 Kings 22:2). The interesting thing about this is that David was not his father. Josiah was 13 generations removed from David, but the generational connection was still valid. Revival came to Israel because Josiah tore down personal and national idols and turned the nation back to the God of their father David.

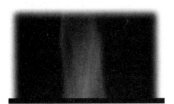

Revival came to Israel because Josiah tore down personal and national idols and turned the nation back to the God of their father David.

From my dream, I knew that God was telling me to be like Hilkiah the priest and connect the next generation of "kings" with God's history of revival and faithfulness. Days later I was given an opportunity when I was asked to give a sermon during Black History week at New Beginnings Church in Fort Worth, Texas. The pastor, without knowing the details of my dream, asked me to speak on February 22—yes, 2-22! Moreover, often in Scripture the number 8, the ages of Josiah when he became king and of the young boy in my dream, represents new beginnings—the name of this church. During the meeting, people were saved and we had a glorious time. For extras, two people were present—an 8-year-old and a 16-year-old—whose birthdays were on February 22. Either that was God or a really bad joke. Some people get signs and wonders; I get street signs and numbers! (I blame it all on Dutch—

I lived a normal life until I met him.)

Apart from stretching my cerebral limits beyond the normal, what might all of this mean to us? God is emphasizing that sometimes we cannot reach for the future until we've been touched by the past. There is a *new beginning* of *kings and priests* today. God wants to connect these kings and priests with the timeless things He did *yesterday* so that they will be enabled to more effectively conceive and birth the *future*. Their connection with the past will empower personal and national destinies— they'll be history makers. We call this the Josiah awakening. As we discuss this, expect something to come alive within you, just as it did in Josiah!

THE GENERATIONS RECONNECTED

In *Digging the Wells of Revival*, Lou Engle writes:

> Strategies alone will never bring revival because revival is the eruption of God's heart on a life poured out. It's the Father's response to those who have been His lovers and to whom He gave promises and sent fire on their offerings. These faithful ones passed into glory and their eternal reward. There then arises another generation, a generation of great grandsons and great granddaughters " . . . who knew neither the Lord nor what He had done for Israel [His people]" (Judges 2:10). One day one of these granddaughters finds a book among the heirlooms and prized possessions of her grandmother stored in the attic. The book is her grandmother's diary, the stories of a woman who prayed hours . . . until the Holy Spirit came and shook her church and

the surrounding township. As the young girl reads, she begins to burn inside, saying, "This is my heritage. Wow!" . . . That young girl pours herself out to God, and another memorial is made.[2]

Lou was using a hypothetical example to describe this reconnecting of the generations, but we know someone to whom this is precisely what happened. Tommi Femrite is a powerful intercessor with an incredible heritage. One day, while rummaging through her grandparents' attic, Tommi found an old prayer diary that had been written by her great-great-great-grandmother five generations earlier. At the time Tommi found it, she was not a Christian, nor were her parents (later she became the first person in her immediate family to get saved). Reading the diary, Tommi learned that she is a descendant of Ruth Bond, who had been an itinerant Quaker preacher during the Civil War.

The first line of this more than 150-year-old historical document says, "I am writing this diary so that my children's, children, children may know the Lord Jesus Christ."[3] In the diary Ruth Bond wrote that at 12 she became sick and died. As she was approaching Heaven, Ruth heard the prayers of her family calling her back home. She wrote how the Lord appeared to her and told her she was not finished on Earth—God called her to preach. She accepted His call, was revived, was totally healed and went on to pursue God's will for her life.

Years after Tommi's conversion she remembered this prayer, was gripped by the memory of Ruth and wanted to study the journal in more detail. Tommi had become a Christian leader and conference speaker, teaching prayer seminars all over the world and founding Gatekeepers International. After going back and looking at her matriarch's diary, she made an incredible discovery: Favorite themes and teachings of Tommi's were themes and teachings Ruth Bond had written about 150 years earlier. Many details, including Scripture references, were the same. For example, Tommi has a teaching series on the Lion of Judah. To her surprise, her great-great-great-grandmother had an extensive teaching in her diary on the Lion of Judah!

Tommi had no prior knowledge of these things. Many generations of Tommi's family didn't know the Lord, but when she connected with the prayers of her matriarch, her life was changed. The lives of the people who have accepted Christ as a result of her ministry have also been changed. That is a Josiah awakening.

A Josiah Connection

Consider the following Josiah connection:

> When George McCluskey married and started a family, he decided to invest one hour a day in prayer, because he wanted his kids to follow Christ. After a time, he expanded his prayers to include his grandchildren and great-grandchildren. Every day between 11:00 A.M. and noon, he prayed for the next three generations. All of these offspring either married a minister, or became one, and were involved in full-time Christian service—all but one, that is. He earned a doctorate, became a psychologist, wrote bestsellers and started a radio show. That man's name is James Dobson![4]

Witness the power of prayer and generational blessing! George McCluskey partnered with God, and God's destiny for his great-grandson James Dobson was realized. You may be saying, "But I don't know if I have a godly heritage. I don't know my history, and nobody in my family has thought to preserve stories or relics from the past." Perhaps not, but you can do as Ruth did when she said to Naomi, "Your people shall be my people and your God, my God" (Ruth 1:16). Though they were not related by blood, Ruth was connecting herself to Naomi and the God of Naomi. And in so doing, she was also connecting to Abraham, Isaac and Jacob and claiming that heritage. Did God honor this connection? It would seem so: Ruth became the great-grandmother of King David! We are talking about *spiritual* inheritance and *spiritual* forebearers. If Christ is in you, He can connect you with past mantles, whether or not you are related by blood to the individuals involved.

Lou Engle and Frank Bartleman

Our good friend Lou Engle, whom we just quoted, gives an account of this kind of reconnecting in his own life. Lou says that after reading Frank Bartleman's account of the Azusa Street Revival—which was led by the African-American preacher William Seymour at the beginning of the twentieth century—his heart was stirred by the passion, the life of prayer and the fasting that Bartleman had lived. He was gripped by how God had used Bartleman to produce revival in Pasadena, Los Angeles and else-where around the nation. At the time of his discovery, Lou had just moved to Pasadena, where Bartleman also had lived. Though Lou is not related to him, he felt a connection with this man of faith and cried out for his mantle. Lou said he cried out to God for hours one day after reading this book, praying, "Lord, give me the mantle for prayer Frank Bartleman had! I want what he had!"[5] This intense intercession went on for about two hours.

Unaware of this, a friend of Lou's came to him the next day and said, "Lou, I had a dream about you last night. In the dream, I was handed a black book with 'Revival' written in gold letters across the front. I opened it up and saw a picture of a man named Frank Bartleman, with his name underneath the picture. As I was looking at the picture, all of a sudden his face changed to yours, Lou!"[6] His friend had no idea that just the day before, Lou had been crying out for Bartleman's mantle for revival. A Josiah awakening was in process!

Lou Engle has since become a spiritual forerunner who has been raised up to lead intercession efforts for another spiritual awakening, and he has helped re-dig the wells of revival in Pasadena. For three years, the church where Lou is an associate pastor, Harvest Rock, met almost daily as it experienced a move of the Spirit that attracted hundreds of thousands of people. Many people were saved and numerous signs and wonders occurred.

Even though past saints are gone, the promises God made to them are not.

Not only did God honor Lou's re-digging of this local well, but He also gave him a national well. Lou has become a voice used by God to gather more than 1 million people to fast and pray in 12-hour-long gatherings, both in America and around the world. The first of these events—known as The Call—took place on the Mall in Washington, D.C. With little advertising and no listing of participants, it attracted more than 400,000 people from all over America. Just as Josiah did with David, by the work of the Holy Spirit, Lou has become the "son" of a man (Frank Bartleman) whom he never met.

Remember that according to Hebrews 11:39-40, even though past saints are gone, the promises God made to them are not. And God wants to empower our today with these promises, many of which are unfulfilled, and allow us to reap the benefits of these saints' faithfulness. He desires to connect us with their legacy, releasing the power of yesterday, creating a generational momentum and finishing what was begun through them. God always builds on what He has done yesterday. He never wastes it.

It is awesome how God uses this synergistic connecting with the past to produce revival. We can only imagine the depth of healing that could have happened had the Azusa Street Revival been fully embraced and not later contaminated by division and strife. However, this mantle is still drifting and waiting for our generation to take up where others left off.

Count Zinzendorf

This same generational connecting occurred with Count Zinzendorf and the Moravians, producing another spiritual awakening. Count Zinzendorf, moved by the 100-year-old writings of Comenius's history of the Moravians, set out to find Moravian refugees and share with them their rich past. Dispersed all over, they gathered one by one at Zinzendorf's place called Herrnhut. By this time, many of them were part of different denominations and doctrinal beliefs and were therefore divided. Deciding to quit arguing about differences, they gathered around the centrality of their union in Christ. They developed a philosophy called *Unitas Fratrum*, or Unity of the Brethren, and this unity created synergy among their diverse group.

Zinzendorf eventually put together the rules of conduct and tenets for the group, called the "manorial rules." One day, Zinzendorf happened to pick up another book by Comenius and was astonished to see that more than 100 years earlier, Comenius had written virtually the same rules of conduct and tenets that Zinzendorf had written. Amazed, he shared this connection with the refugees, and this providential linking had a profound effect on the group. "Not only were they growing in unity with each other, but the count's discovery at Zitau made them now feel a genuine link and a sense of unity with the saints who had gone before them."[7] Another Josiah awakening was occurring.

The expectation level and anticipation of a move of the Spirit among them went throughout Herrnhut. On Wednesday, August 13, 1727, while in prayer, the Holy Spirit fell in great power in what has been described as the Moravian Pentecost. One Moravian testified, "We discovered therein the finger of God, and found ourselves as it were, baptized under the cloud of our fathers, with their spirit. For that Spirit came again upon us, and great signs and wonders were wrought among the Brethren in those days, and great grace prevailed among us, and in the whole country."[8]

This began the now-famous, 100-year-long continuous prayer meeting that launched modern missions and the first Great Awakening! Josiah awakenings make history! The saints burned with such a great evangelistic flame that they even sold themselves into slavery in order to share the gospel in different nations. Their synergistic agreement with one another and their past brought a supernatural, exponential, multiplied release of the power of the Holy Spirit. Maybe it was because God remembered His friend Comenius. Count Zinzendorf was used like a Hilkiah to connect the Moravians to their past, and like Josiah they brought revival and shaped the future. One hundred years of barrenness had been redeemed as God breathed upon dry bones and replaced the spiritual decay with 100 years of night-and-day prayer that birthed great awakenings!

The Ivy League

On our prayer journey, the Kettle Tour, we visited many of the places in the Northeast that had been touched by these awakenings. We went to re-dig the wells of revival and ask for the ancient pathways of righteousness in our nation. Part of our God-given assignment was to go to Ivy League universities and college campuses to break the stronghold of false ideologies that had come through the French Enlightenment (the idolatrous worship of knowledge and man: humanism) and to pray for the turning of our nation's educational system to God. Many of these schools, such as Harvard, Princeton, Yale and Dartmouth, began as Christian schools, and most had been powerfully impacted by revival.

Lou Engle had actually been challenged by a United States senator to go to Harvard, unclog the wells of revival and break false ideologies that existed there. After praying at Harvard during the day, I (Dutch) sensed that we needed to go back that night to pray again—sort of like Gideon's night strike. Gideon once asked, "Where are the power and the miracles our forefathers saw?" (see Judg. 6:13). He, like Josiah, reconnected to his God-given heritage, even though his father was a worshiper of Baal. In Judges 6:25-27, Gideon went at night to tear down his father's altar of idolatry and, in its place, built an altar to the Lord, turning Israel back to the God of their fathers.

Not knowing exactly where to go, we went around the perimeter of this huge campus, which was surrounded by a 12-foot-high fence that had most of the gates closed. We thought we would have to pray from outside the fence, but we eventually came upon an open gate and went inside the campus. We had no idea what part of the campus we were in and didn't really know where to stop to pray. There were several buildings nearby, and we wondered if one might be significant to our assignment. As we wandered around, a team member noticed that one of the buildings had an inscription and story with which I was familiar. (I actually share about this in *The River of God*.) During the construction of this building, Emerson Hall, the president of Harvard, Charles Eliot, asked a noted psychologist and philosopher to suggest a suitable inscription. The suggested quote, from the Greek philosopher Protagoras: "Man is the measure of all things."[9]

Eliot, a strong Christian, refused to use this humanistic phrase. It wasn't until the scaffolding and canvas were removed from the construction site that it became apparent the president had chosen to have Psalm 8:4 inscribed on the building instead. It says, "What is man that Thou art mindful of him?" Eliot's choice from the psalmist shows the great difference between God-centered and human-centered points of view.[10] How amazing that God led our Kettle Tour group to this specific location!

We prayed discreetly, proclaiming the tearing down of the strongholds of humanism that have clogged this righteous well. We agreed with Harvard's former president Charles Eliot, and asked God for a shift in the educational system of America. Lou Engle powerfully prayed all of Psalm 8, which ends with the words "O LORD our Lord, how excellent is thy name in all the earth!" (v. 9, *KJV*).

All of our Ivy-League-school prayer times seemed very key and extremely powerful. About six months after the tour, we received a report from a campus ministry saying, "Many people do not understand why, but there has been a revival of prayer at many of the Ivy League schools in the nation. Brown, Cornell, Yale and other schools have noticed an increase in campus prayer meetings and Bible studies. At Princeton, 500 Christian students are meeting and praying for the other 4,500 who are not saved."[11]

About the same time, we received a report from a Harvard University student.

We have never seen so much prayer on the Harvard campus:

- For the first time, a group of intercessors from 62 countries (the Joshua Project) is coming together on a weekly basis to pray for revival at Harvard.
- For the first time, eight graduate fellowships have united to pray weekly for revival at Harvard.
- For the first time in recent history, both graduates and undergraduates gathered to pray all night for Harvard, and some 60 students and intercessors from the community turned up.
- People are getting saved and baptized in the Holy Spirit on the Harvard campus, "seven in our fellowship alone this past year," said one student. During last week's "revival" services at the Memorial Church, many people came forward to be prayed for, and at least 10 to 20 people accepted Christ.
- For the first time, both undergraduate and graduate Christians have united for an all-campus worship and prayer—packing a 300-seat auditorium. People had to sit on the carpet.
- Many relationships have been formed this year with local churches, and pastors all over the Boston region are leading their congregations in prayer for Harvard.[12]

Something was stirred at these schools and others in 2001 and 2002. We believe the reconnecting to the covenants of their forefathers is one important action that is impacting them. As we continue to pray, let's ask God to give us these ancient pathways, making our schools revival centers again.

DRY BONES AND PROMISES

Centuries ago, Josiah looked out over his nation Israel and saw the same dry bones that Ezekiel saw in the valley (see Ezek. 37:1-10). The dry bones represented an apostate Israel, spiritually dead. Through a mighty outpouring of the Holy Spirit the dry bones were resurrected and became an army. Can it happen again right here in America? Can't you just hear the aching heart of a passionate God saying to His covenant friends, "Can these dry bones live?"

There are 3 billion to 4 billion of these spiritual skeletons scattered throughout the earth. Millions of them in this apostate nation are disguised as teenagers, retirees, yuppies, buppies, gangbangers, humanists, feminists, New Agers, Muslims, Buddhists, atheists, liberals, conservatives and every other cloak you can imagine. They are hungry and thirsty, spiritually dead but looking for life. And they can live!

The Momentum of History

It is time for us to connect with past mantles and anointings. It is time to lay hold of past promises and prayers until the momentum of history crashes onto the shores of America today. A synergistic joining of generations, races and believers from every walk of life must occur, producing exponential ramifications once again. It is time.

If we do this, it will not only affect today but it will also affect tomorrow. We too can leave legacies that stir God's heart to act for our offspring. What if Will's kettle had been passed down without the story? It would be just another old pot. But someone took the responsibility to pass down the history. Let's remember history—and make history. We must steward the promises made to our forefathers so that we too will have something to pass on. It is time for us to lift up a cry that God cannot deny, reminding Him of our righteous predecessors, and to ask for another great awakening in America.

Our Greatest Legacy

The story is told of Louis Pasteur, the famous French scientist who was the inventor of many things, one of them being the rabies vaccine. He lived at a time when thousands of people were dying of rabies. Pasteur had just developed the vaccine and was about to try it on himself when a mother brought in her son who was dying of this dreaded disease. Pasteur opted instead to try it on the young lad for 10 days. The 9-year-old boy, Joseph Meister, was miraculously cured and lived. Louis Pasteur went on to have several other inventions that were very noteworthy and greatly contributed to society. When he died, of all the things he could have placed on his epitaph, Pasteur requested only three words: Joseph Meister lived.

We too can leave legacies that stir God's heart to act for our offspring.

, Our greatest legacy will be those who live eternally because of our efforts. May we truly be God's covenantal friends, and through this cause a generation of dry bones to realize their God-given destinies, inoculated with the resurrection power of

Almighty God. When history books mention us, let it be said that we were a Josiah generation of prophetic voices who connected with our fathers and reformed a nation. May it be said that when everyone else saw hopeless dry bones, we saw an army and, like Ezekiel, prophesied life to our generation. On our memorial stones let our epitaph read: The dry bones lived.

> *Father, thank You for the greater works, the spiritual blessing and inheritance we have in Jesus. Oh, God, let the well of our yesterday be released today. Where is the God of Elijah, William Seymour and Count Zinzendorf? Let Your passions erupt now on us—their offspring—that we may declare Your works to future generations. And through our agreement, bring about a synergy so powerful that it changes and heals history. Father, break off false ideologies and humanistic thinking from every school, college and university. We agree with Charles Eliot that we are not the center of all things, You are! We speak to the dry bones and say the cloaks are coming off, and new garments are coming! Breath is coming to them, and they will live! An army of Josiahs and Hilkiahs are on the way and we thank You for it. Release generational blessings, and cut off the curses in our family. We ask that future generations in our family would know Christ so that those yet to be created may praise You. Give them a sense of destiny at an early age, just as eight-year-old king Josiah had. Give us a history with You to pass on to them. In Jesus' name, amen.[13]*

Notes

1. Historians in Williamsburg claim that the church led by the Pamphlets was the first black church in America. Others have concluded that a Baptist congregation located near the Georgia-South Carolina border in

the general vicinity of Savannah, Georgia, was the first. Both churches likely started within a few years of each other.

2. Lou Engle, *Digging the Wells of Revival* (Shippensburg, PA: Destiny Image, 1999), p. 60.

3. Tommi Femrite, "Redigging the Wells of Intercession" (lecture, Intercessors International Conference, November 9, 2001).

4. Dutch Sheets, *The Beginner's Guide to Intercessory Prayer* (Ann Arbor, MI: Servant Publications, 2001), p. 84.

5. Lou Engle, unititled (lecture, Transformation Florida: First Session, Winter Haven, FL, January 25, 2002).

6. Ibid.

7. Edward K. Rowell, *Fresh Illustrations for Preaching and Teaching* (Grand Rapids, MI: Baker Books, 1997), p. 90.

8. Ibid.

9. Source unknown.

10. Source unknown.

11. Unidentified student, e-mail dated March 5, 2002.

12. Unidentified student, e-mail dated April 22, 2002.

13. See John 14:12; 2 Kings 2:14; Ezekiel 37:4-14; 2 Kings 22; Psalm 78:6.

Chapter 9

THE INVITATION

Then I will set the key of the house of David on his shoulder, when he opens no one will shut, when he shuts no one will open. I will drive him like a peg in a firm place, and he will become a throne of glory to his father's house. So they will hang on him all the glory of his father's house, offspring and issue, all the least of vessels, from bowls to all the jars. In that day," declares the LORD of hosts, "the peg driven in a firm place will give way; it will even break off and fall, and the load hanging on it will be cut off, for the LORD has spoken."

ISAIAH 22:22-25

I (Dutch) have been smitten by this thought: *We can either watch history being made, or we can make it.* A few years ago on my birthday, a friend gave me a beautiful pen inscribed with the words "History Maker." Will I really become one? We'll know in 20 or

30 years. But I can assure you of one thing—I'm going to spend my life investing in the process. Being a history maker sometimes results in the sacrifice of our time, money and comforts in order to respond to the invitations God gives us. A halfhearted reply or no response to our epoch-making opportunity can be costly.

Our friend Chris Bergland had a dream that illustrates this point. In his dream, he was handed a book of history. The first section consisted of people who had received beautiful invitations from the Lord. The individuals showed off the invitations to others and then placed them in ornate treasure boxes. However, they never attended the occasion or did what the invitation asked. The page would turn, and their next page of history would be blank. The next section of the book included people who had received invitations from the Lord and responded to the opportunity with acts of obedience. Powerful consequences—revivals and strategic victories in history—followed as a result of their partnering with God. The last page was about a prayer gathering: two outcomes were listed on opposite sides of the same page. One side read, "Nice Gathering Yields 30-Fold Fruit." The flipside of the page read, "Historic Gathering Sends Shockwaves Around the World!"

WINDOWS OF OPPORTUNITY

The interpretation of Chris's dream was that God is giving out invitations to write history. Not responding can result in a blank page. A casual response can yield very little fruit. However, the good news is that a wholehearted embrace of God's invitation can shape history and send shockwaves around the world. This illustrates how tragic it is to receive an invitation from the Lord and respond lethargically or not at all.

In this dream, it seems that those in the first section treasured the invitation more than the opportunity! How many times do we flaunt our treasure box of invitations (dreams, revelation, new positions and titles), using them only to promote ourselves as we boast to others? While our next page remains blank, the God of history longingly awaits our obedient reply. Basically, the Lord is asking, "Who will accept the invitation and buy the opportunity?"

Twice the New Testament says to redeem the time (see Eph. 5:15-17; Col. 4:5, *KJV*). "To redeem" is *exagorazo*, meaning "buy" or "purchase." "Time" is *kairos*, meaning "opportune, epoch-making time." Buy the opportunity! Yes, opportunities must be bought. They cost something: time, energy, abilities, money, our very lives. If we don't spend what is necessary and buy them, opportunities can also be lost. The windows won't stay open forever.

A Key of Authority

I (Dutch) received an invitation from the Lord in October 2000 to partner with Him in praying forth His desires for America. God began a remarkable series of confirmations in my life regarding the authority that He wanted to release strategically to the church in America. This had to do with prayer for the presidential election, but it was not limited to that situation. This amazing series of confirmations revealed to me that God was giving us an invitation to move into a new realm of governmental authority. By using the phrase "governmental authority," I am referring to releasing the rule or dominion of God from Heaven to Earth. This would include, as was the case in my life, but not be limited to releasing it over the realm of human government.

The confirmations began on a cross-country flight. I noticed that my departure was at 2:22 P.M. I was seated in row number 22, and the total travel time was 2 hours and 22 minutes. My first thought was, *What an interesting coincidence!* Then the Lord reminded me that He had been speaking to me from Isaiah 22:22: "I will set the key of the house of David on his shoulder, when he opens no one will shut, when He shuts, no one will open." I wondered, *Would God orchestrate something like this to bring me confirmation?*

A few days later I received a phone call from a spiritual father who told me that while in prayer he felt impressed to call and give me Isaiah 22:22. He emphasized the aspect of the key, which represents authority. Then he said, "Dutch, God is giving you a key of authority in this nation." Overall, the Lord gave me at least 25 undeniable confirmations during this season that the Church was to operate in a new realm of governmental authority. Will had similar occurrences.

Confirmations

I (Will) was somewhat skeptical after hearing about Dutch's 22s, as I also was of others who spoke of having similar experiences. That is, until it started happening to me. I began to wake up at 2:22 A.M. At first I thought it was psychosomatic, but it wasn't. One of the numerous ways that God confirmed this was through my own family. I have a niece named Ayanna Fowler who was a student at George Washington University at that time. (She has since graduated.) God began to draw my attention to her in prayer, and the phone rang. I missed picking up the phone, but when I looked on my caller ID to see who had phoned me, it was Ayanna—and the time that she called was 2:22 P.M. I felt that I was supposed to invite her to a prayer gathering in New England, so I called her back. The date for the event had changed, and I called to let her know that it was now on September 22.

She replied, "That's my birthday." I said, "No way! How old will you be?" She said, "Twenty-two years old." Then, when I told her that I needed her address to send her some information, she told me that she had moved off campus and that her apartment address was 2222 Eye Street!

Did God make my niece move just to give me a confirmation? Probably not. Did He plan a prayer event on her birthday, a twenty-second day of a month, to confirm something to me? Not likely. A more plausible explanation is that in His sovereignty and omniscience He takes times, events or places which correlate in such a way that they *could* present confirming patterns. Then He supernaturally weaves them into a series of happenings that absolutely *do* become confirmations. He did this for us where Isaiah 22:22 was concerned.

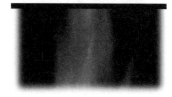

An invitation has gone out, calling forth a new, diverse, unified remnant to decree breakthrough in America.

The Call to Shape History

This confirmation wasn't just for us. An invitation has gone out, calling forth a new, diverse, unified remnant to decree breakthrough in America, shifting this nation back on course. Our desire through this chapter is that you accept the invitation, understand our inherited keys of authority and gain a new understanding of kingly decrees. We must see how different generations are pegged, or given assignments, to shift nations back on track. We can and must seize our *kairos*, epoch-making opportunity to shape history with Him.

You may be wondering, *What exactly is Isaiah 22:22 about?* To get a more complete understanding, let's briefly look at the full context in Isaiah 22:15-25. This passage is talking about Shebna's demotion from being the royal steward for King Hezekiah's household because God was displeased with his abuse of office. "Shebna" means "youthfulness" and as is often the case when one is given authority prematurely, he represents immature, selfish authority. Shebna, like Haman, Herod and others, abused his authority to make a name for himself, lived lavishly and disregarded the next generation.

God said that He was raising up Eliakim, son of Hilkiah, to take his place (see Isa. 22:20). "Eliakim" means "set up," or "raised up by God," and has the connotation of rising after being awakened. His name can literally be translated as "God of awakening." That's what we're looking for! "Hilkiah," the name of his father, means "God is my portion," or "inheritance." Because Hilkiah made God his portion, Eliakim became a son of awakening who inherited keys of authority and was set up as steward of the king's royal household. Wow!

As part of this transfer of authority, Eliakim received Shebna's robe, sash and the key of David (see Isa. 22:21-22), which was a key placed on his shoulder. The shoulder in Scripture conveys the concept of government (see Isa. 9:6). This key shows Eliakim's access to the king, along with authority and stewardship of the royal treasury. This is all meaningful for us. We have been given the key to the kingdom of Heaven (see Matt. 16:19). Figuratively, for us also, the key depicts heavenly access to intimacy with our King and prayer that releases governmental authority, shutting the door to the enemy and opening the door to God's kingdom rule.

You should want that key!

The Throne of Glory

Isaiah 22:23-24 then says that Eliakim was going to represent a throne of glory, driven like a peg in a firm place in his father's house, on which greater and lesser vessels—bowls and jars—would be hung. Bear with us while we get a little detailed and explain the symbolism here. It will be helpful. According to Freeman's *Manners and Customs of the Bible*, the peg mentioned in this context wasn't a tent peg.[1] Rather, it was a special peg in the wall of a house. People actually built the wall around the peg to make sure that it stayed securely in place. Choice bowls and utensils were placed on it. Figuratively, the bowls could represent the prayer bowls in Heaven. The vessels would be people—as in Scripture, people are symbolically vessels and clay jars (see 2 Cor. 4:7; 2 Tim. 2:21). In the text, the jars represent family members of Eliakim's household, Israel, who was depending on him, *the* peg. Isaiah 22:25 shows that in the end, Shebna, the unfaithful steward, was removed and utterly destroyed, along with those who had alliances with him.

What we have here is an awesome picture of our Lord Himself and His Church. Because David made God his portion, he was promised a special descendant to sit on his throne. David was allowed to be a forefather to God's Son of inheritance, Jesus Christ. At the Cross, keys and authority were transferred to Him, and the government now rests on His shoulder (see Isa. 9:6). As the name of Eliakim pictures, Christ is the Son of awakening who died and rose again and is now set up on a throne of glory in His heavenly Father's house (see Ps. 110). He is the One upon whom our prayers rest, the sure peg upon which our salvation depends. We are the jars, family members of the household of faith, who place our trust in Him. Revelation 3:7 confirms this, quoting Isaiah 22:22 and stating that Jesus has been given the key of David.

David himself was given a futuristic glimpse of the coming Messiah and His Church, which he recorded in Psalm 110. We can only imagine the awe and excitement that David must have felt being connected to such a great lineage. You and I should be just as excited. If we're Christians, we are His jars—earthen vessels filled with the treasure of God Himself (see 2 Cor. 4:7). This is our inheritance, and because of it, we're invited to partner in ruling and reigning with Christ.

The Feet of Jesus

Psalm 110 foretells that Christ would sit at the right hand of the Father. According to the New Testament, at the time of this ascension and enthronement, He had *already* placed all other authorities under His feet.

> And He put all things in subjection under His feet, and gave Him as head over all things to the church (Eph. 1:22).

> For He has put all things in subjection under His feet. But when He says, "All things are put in subjection," it is evident that He is excepted who put all things in subjection to Him (1 Cor. 15:27).

But Psalm 110 informs us that after His ascension He would still be *waiting* for His enemies to become His footstool: "Sit at My right hand, *until* I make Your enemies a footstool for Your feet" (Ps. 110:1, emphasis added).

But wait a minute. Do we have a contradiction between this Messianic prophecy and the New Testament verses that say that after He ascended to the Father's right hand they were *already* under His feet? No. Then why the seeming inconsistency? Since

He has ascended, *are* they under His feet or *will* they be placed there? The answer is YES! They are *legally* there through the Cross. They will be *literally* placed there as we do our part. Psalm 110:2-3 goes on to describe our part:

> The LORD will stretch forth Your strong scepter from Zion, saying, "Rule in the midst of Your enemies." Your people will volunteer freely in the day of Your power; in holy array, from the womb of the dawn, Your youth are to You as the dew.

An Army of Volunteers

The word "power" in this passage, *chayil,* is also translated "army." Christ will use an army of volunteers who will stretch forth His strong scepter of authority, ruling in the midst of their enemies and enforcing His great victory. When they do, His enemies become His footstool.

The volunteer army of Queen Esther's day models this for us in the Old Testament. This fatherless girl, Esther, and her cousin, Mordecai, changed the fate of a nation by responding to the invitation and buying the opportunity (see Esther 4:14). Haman, enemy of the Jews, persuaded the king to make a decree that all the Jews were to be annihilated on a certain day (see Esther 3:7-11). Esther, the queen, knew she must do something. But knowing that the penalty was death for appearing before the king without having been summoned, Esther called for three days of corporate fasting before she went to meet with him (see Esther 4:16). Favor resulted and Esther was extended the king's scepter (see Esther 5:2-3).

Eventually Esther held two banquets that brought her even greater favor with the king. She and Mordecai received the king's authority to decree a command which, in effect, reversed

Haman's plot and released justice on the Jews' behalf (see Esther 7:1-6; 8:8). They accepted their invitation when God's scepter was extended to them. We must do the same.

As the Body of Christ, we are His Bride and the concept of a bride speaks of intimacy. But we also hold His scepter of authority. We are His war bride—just as Esther was with her king—and the Lord invites us to decree His purposes on Earth. Accept the invitation and become a volunteer. Let's look at a modern day example of this.

An Example: Saddam Hussein

The Lord assembled a portion of His volunteer prayer army in Texas to stretch forth His scepter and decree the capture of Saddam Hussein. First, please understand that we are not so naive as to think we are the sole reason for Saddam's capture. Nor do we think that prayer is like magical fairy dust and with it we can make just anything happen at will. Many sincere prayers have been prayed by families for the safety of their sons and daughters who are in the military, yet sometimes in times of war there are casualties. We have prayed for the capture of Osama bin Laden and, as of the writing of this book, our prayers have not yet been answered. There are some questions about prayer that are way beyond our explanation and comprehension. Deuteronomy 29:29 says, "The secret things belong to the LORD our God, but the things revealed belong to us and to our sons forever, that we may observe all the words of this law." Although some things are hidden from us, this verse says that the revealed things belong to us for our instruction.

On December 8 and December 9, 2003, in San Antonio, Texas, Will and I participated in a strategic prayer time, calling forth the army of the Lord in Texas. This gathering was part of a

50-state prayer tour, led by Chuck Pierce and me. We toured the nation, gathering intercessors in each state to pray for revival in America. Because this gathering was held on a Monday and a Tuesday, many thought that maybe 400 to 500 people would show up; instead, more than 1,500 people attended this historic prayer time.

Honestly, we didn't go to pray specifically about the war in Iraq. We went to minister to the Lord and follow His leading just as we did in each state. Messianic Jews, Native Americans, Hispanics, African Americans, Asians and Caucasians were present and played key roles in the prayer time. There was a true synergy of God's people. His presence and His blessing were very evident as we worshiped and offered up prayers of petition and repentance. We asked

God was so honored by the brokenness, unity and agreement that He allowed us to move *from the censer to the scepter.*

God, and one another, to forgive the sins of racism, and we also petitioned the Lord to forgive Texas as a state for the corporate sins of the people and the government.

From the Censer to the Scepter

God was so honored by the brokenness, unity and agreement that He allowed us to move *from the censer to the scepter*. Priests use censers. Kings use scepters. We moved from functioning in priestly intercession—praise, repentance and petition—to kingly intercession as well—authoritative proclamation and decrees.

During prayer, Chuck Pierce began to proclaim, "Texas, the Lord would say to you that there is a nation in your loins." Shortly after this was said, a pastor came forward and said, "I believe the Lord has just shown me what nation is in our loins, and that nation is Iraq. . . . We need to pray for the 4th Infantry Division out of Fort Hood, Texas." This prayer meeting took place during the war with Iraq, before Saddam Hussein was found. This pastor went on to explain how key the 4th Infantry Division was, because it was one of several divisions tracking and looking for Hussein. Chuck actually prophesied that "in this state tonight you will be able to decree to Babylon and that strongman that has not been found will now be found, saith the Lord."

Chuck and I began to lead in decrees for the exposure and finding of Saddam and began to pray against all witchcraft that was keeping him hidden. As these decrees went forth, tears fell and shouts and travailing could be heard from those present. This was definitely not something born of our own wills but was a sovereign invitation to partner with God—to take the keys of Isaiah 22:22 and govern! Our prayer time ended with an African-American, uniformed military officer's coming forward and praying, "As a witness to the prophetic word in this house, as a representative of the armed forces in the state of Texas, I declare in the name of the Lord, it shall be." All of these things were done with the obvious leading of the Holy Spirit and with great boldness. We knew that our prayers would be answered, but, honestly, I was a little surprised at how bold we had become.

An Answer to Prayer

At the end of that week, on Saturday, December 13, 2003, I (Will) received a phone call from my friend Mike Holloway. Without knowing about our prayer gathering, he said, "Will, you've been talking to me about the book of Esther, and I thought I'd read it today. When I picked up my Bible, it opened to Esther 9:1, which says,

Now in the twelfth month, that is, the month of Adar, on the thirteenth day, the time came for the king's command and his decree to be executed. On the day that the enemies of the Jews had hoped to overpower them, the opposite occurred, in that the Jews themselves overpowered those who hated them (*NKJV*).

"The passage goes on to say that it was the same day that Haman's sons were found and brought to justice on the gallows that had been made for the Jews," Mike continued. "Today is the twelfth month and the thirteenth day. We need to pray—something is going on!"[2]

I didn't really connect our conversation with our previous prayer time in San Antonio, but Mike has had a track record of being prophetic and I knew something significant was happening. Everything made sense the following morning.

Early on Sunday morning I received a call from Dutch, who told me to turn on my television, because Saddam Hussein had been captured! As the story unfolded, I was amazed to learn that the 4th Infantry Division from Fort Hood, which we had prayed for, was the division that had found him and that Hussein had been caught the previous day, Saturday, *the thirteenth day of the twelfth month.*

As providence would have it, Iraq was formerly part of Babylon, where Esther had lived. Hussein was known for his mass annihilation and brutality, and it could be said that a new son of Haman, Saddam Hussein, was found and brought to justice on the twelfth month and the thirteenth day—just like Haman's sons of old. The Lord released shockwaves on the other side of the world in Iraq, at least in part, because a remnant had responded wholeheartedly to the invitation to shape history.

Priestly Intercession

Revelation 5:10 is a relevant verse. It says, "And hast made us unto our God kings and priests: and we shall reign on the earth" (*KJV*). This verse says we are both kings and priests. As such, God is giving us the understanding and ability, more and more, to move from the censer to the scepter in prayer. In other words, we move from priestly prayer to kingly declaration. The censer was the bowl in which incense was burned, representing the priestly function of praise, repentance, prayer and worship before the Lord. Priests filled the holy of holies with the smoke of incense from the censer, as they offered up petitions on behalf of the people.

The scepter represents the rule of the king and also the extension of his power. It releases his favor, judgment or decree. When we pray, we often move from one function to the other—from the censer to the scepter.

This pattern can be seen in the Lord's Prayer. The phrases, "Our Father, which art in heaven, hallowed be Your name;" "give us this day our daily bread;" "forgive us our trespasses;" and "lead us not into temptation;" are examples of our offering up to God prayers, praise, repentance and requests concerning the needs of humankind. The book of Hebrews describes this aspect of Jesus' prayer life. The writer of Hebrews says, "During the days of Jesus' life on earth, he *offered up prayers* and *petitions* with loud cries and tears" (5:7, *NIV*, emphasis added). This is priestly intercession.

However, with the words "Thy kingdom come, Thy will be done on earth as it is in heaven," we shift into a declaration—kingly intercession. In the original Greek, this kingly portion is not a request, it is a command! It could be rephrased, "Thy kingdom, come! Will of God, be done!" The words "be done" come from the Greek word *ginomai*, which also means "to create." Releasing decrees, when led by the Holy Spirit to do so, creates the will of God on Earth. Jesus modeled this in John 11:11-43. Because He knew the heart of the Father, He used the key of David to reverse the verdict of death against Lazarus. When Jesus the Son of Awakening decreed, "Lazarus, come forth," the will of God was *ginomai-ed*. His keys of authority opened the tomb door and life was created (see John 11:43)! Christ has extended keys to us, calling us to enter into the same relationship. As priests we are invited to offer up prayers to Heaven; but once we have the mind of the Lord, as kings we release His decrees from Heaven to Earth. We are called to do this individually and collectively. Ezra 9:8 says, "But now for a brief moment grace has been shown from the LORD our God, to leave us an escaped remnant and to give us a peg in His holy place, that our God may enlighten our eyes and grant us a little reviving in our bondage." This collective remnant was pegged to steward Israel's awakening, being revived to repair the ruins of their nation.

The Breaking of Slavery and Racism

Throughout the history of America, we can see that different generations were pegged, or given invitations, to steward awakenings for God. They were used to open the eyes of this nation to its true moral-heart condition and heal it. Whether they knew it or not, they moved in the authority of Isaiah 22 and Psalm 110, mixing kingly and priestly anointings. They were extended favor with the King and used their keys of authority to change the nation. The God of Awakening (Eliakim) tipped the bowls of prayer. As a result there were mass conversions, powerful signs and wonders, healings of all kinds and the greatest injustice of that day—slavery—was broken.

Later, through Dr. Martin Luther King, Jr., in the 1960s, America was awakened to the injustice of segregation and Jim Crow laws.[3] Favor rested on Dr. King and a generation of believers, and the bowls of Heaven were tipped in their behalf. They were pegged by God to shift the courts in America.

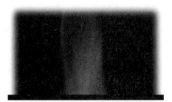

The generation of Martin Luther King, Jr., was given a key that opened the door to a floodgate of justice.

The generation of Martin Luther King, Jr., was given a key that opened the door to a floodgate of justice that rolled like a mighty river, and righteousness came like an ever-flowing stream. Dr. King said that fasting and prayer were what gave him the power to do what he did to change the nation. God gave people the grace to turn the other cheek as they were stoned, beaten with sticks and clubs, falsely accused and jailed, and sometimes killed. Although most white churches didn't get involved, a remnant of white believers prayed and marched alongside their black brothers and sisters. Some, such as Reverend Bruce Klunder, were martyred along with them as well.

Dr. King's words "Injustice anywhere is a threat to justice everywhere,"[4] still ring through the ages. He exposed how segregation devalued the life of African Americans and said that denying their existence and right to all parts of society was unjust and inhumane. Dr. King was an Eliakim who used keys of awakening to release justice, bringing us all closer to his God-given dream.

SUCH A TIME AS THIS

I (Will) believe that with the key of David our Christian forefathers in the 1800s opened the door to revival and shut the door to legalized slavery. Another generation furthered the cause of racial justice. And I believe that now their mantle and keys of authority are being extended through the ages to this generation, to open the door to revival and shut the door to unjust courts again. Surely, one of our assignments is to contend for the covenants our forefathers made with God and pray in the awakening that will break off this decree of death from our nation. The same God who broke the power of Dred Scott and Jim Crow laws is inviting us to pray in a revival that will break the power of *Roe v. Wade*. Like He did with fatherless Esther, who broke Haman's decree to kill the Jews, God has betrothed Himself to a fatherless Esther generation that has been pegged and called to the kingdom for such a time as this. He is marrying and joining races, denominations and movements together to be a synergistic peg that will have keys of authority in this nation.

Our generation is being given access to Isaiah 22:22 keys that will birth God's desires, shut doors of darkness and open doors to life and justice. Prayer bowls from generations before have been poured on us, empowering us to complete what was started in their day. Generations after us are the clay jars that will be the recipients of our obedience. As President George W. Bush said after September 11, 2001, "The commitment of our fathers has become the calling of our time."[5]

A broken, diverse, unified remnant in the Body of Christ can change the world, much the same way that Esther's generation did. Walter Wink said, "History belongs to the intercessor."[6] We agree. Winston Churchill once said, "History will be kind to me, for I intend to write it."[7] This is your invitation. Be the pen in the hand of God. Allow Christ to write a love letter through the history you make. Let Him heal the past and shape the future with your life of intercession and obedience. What an exciting time to be alive! You're a history maker who has been called to the Kingdom for such a time as this.

Accept the invitation!

> *Father, I thank You that Your Son of inheritance, Jesus Christ,*
> *has the key of David. Thank You that what He opens no one*
> *shuts, and what He shuts no one opens. And by the authority*
> *given me in His name, I approach You now. I accept Your invi-*
> *tation, knowing I've been called into the Kingdom for such a*
> *time as this, to enter into a deeper place of intimacy and reign-*
> *ing with You. Raise up the Eliakims and Esthers. Tip bowls of*
> *prayer and break the decrees of Shebna, Herod and Hamon*
> *over a fatherless generation. That which began in previous gen-*
> *erations, let it be completed through us. I receive my invitation*
> *to write history with You. May the accumulated prayers be*
> *downloaded on me and a generation pegged for Your glory. In*
> *Jesus' name, amen.*[8]

Notes

1. James M. Freeman, *Manners and Customs of the Bible* (Plainfield, NJ: Logos International, 1987), p. 263.
2. Mike Holloway, phone conversation with Will Ford, December 13, 2003.
3. The Dred Scott legal decision ruled that slaves had no rights. It was similar to *Roe v. Wade* that declared that the unborn have no rights. Named for a minstrel show character, Jim Crow laws were late-nineteenth-century statutes passed by the legislatures of the Southern states, creating a racial caste system in the American South. After the end of slavery, in the city, blacks and whites were in more direct competition than they had been in the countryside. The Jim Crow laws were a response to a new reality that required white supremacy to move to where it would have a rigid legal and institutional basis to retain control over the black population. In the city, blacks and whites were in more direct competition than they had been in the countryside. There was more danger of social mixing. The city, there-fore, required different, and more rigidly institutionalized, systems of

control. In 1883, The U.S. Supreme Court began to strike down the foundations of the post-Civil War Reconstruction, declaring the Civil Rights Act of 1875 unconstitutional. The Court also ruled that the Fourteenth Amendment prohibited state governments from discriminating against people because of race but did not restrict private organizations or individuals from doing so. The high court rulings led to a profusion of Jim Crow laws. The Supreme Court, in 1896, legitimized the principle of "separate but equal" in its ruling *Plessy v. Ferguson*. The Court held that separate accommodations did not deprive blacks of equal rights if the accommodations were equal. In 1899, the Court went even further declaring in *Cumming v. County Board of Education*: Laws establishing separate schools for whites were valid even if they provided no comparable schools for blacks. By 1914 every Southern state had passed laws that created two separate societies; one black, the other white. Blacks and whites could not ride together in the same railroad cars, sit in the same waiting rooms, use the same washrooms, eat in the same restaurants, or sit in the same theaters. Blacks were denied access to parks, beaches and picnic areas; they were barred from many hospitals. [Dr. Charles Drew, the inventor of blood plasma, died in need of the very plasma he created. An African American, he was injured in a car wreck and couldn't go to the nearest hospital because of his race. He died on the way to the hospital that treated Negroes]. The first major blow against the Jim Crow system of racial segregation was struck in 1954 by the Supreme Court's decision in *Brown v. Board of Education* of Topeka, Kansas, which declared segregation in the public schools unconstitutional. [This Christian-led, student movement broke the back of school segregation]. This began what is known as the "Civil Rights Movement" and began the end of the Jim Crow laws.

4. Martin Luther King, Jr., *Quote DB*. http://www.quotedb.com/quotes/47 (accessed June 9, 2004).

5. George W. Bush, "President's Remarks at National Day of Prayer and Remembrance," (speech, The National Cathedral, Washington, D.C., September 14, 2001), *White House*. http://www.whitehouse.gov/news/releases/2001/09/20010914-2.html (accessed March 30, 2004).

6. Walter Wink, *Engaging The Powers: Discernment and Resistance in a World of Domination* (Minneapolis, MN: Fortress Press, 1992), p. 298.

7. Winston Churchill, quoted at *BrainyQuote*. http://www.brainyquote.com/quotes/quotes/w/winstonchu100132.html (accessed June 9, 2004).

8. See Revelation 3:7; Isaiah 22:15-25; Esther 4:14; Psalm 110.

THE GOD OF OUR INHERITANCE

by Will Ford

But he went in and stood before his master. And Elisha said to him,
"Where have you been, Gehazi?" And he said, "Your servant went
nowhere." Then he said to him, "Did not my heart go with you, when
the man turned from his chariot to meet you? Is it a time to receive
money and to receive clothes and olive groves and vineyards and sheep
and oxen and male and female servants? Therefore, the leprosy of
Naaman shall cling to you and to your descendants forever." So he
went out from his presence a leper as white as snow.

2 KINGS 5:25-27

One aspect of synergistic agreement that God is restoring is
the spiritual father-mother and son-daughter relationships in
the Body of Christ. In Romans 16:21, Paul says, "Timothy my
fellow worker greets you, and so do Lucius and Jason and
Sosipater, my kinsmen." The Timothy to whom Paul is referring is his spiritual son, to whom he wrote two mentoring letters before he died (see 1 Tim. and 2 Tim.). The words "fellow
worker" in this Scripture come from the Greek word *sunergos*,
from which we derive our English word "synergy." There is a
synergy released through spiritual fathers and mothers to spiritual sons and daughters that causes exponentially powerful
relationships.

God is renewing the importance of these relationships in
our day. The hearts of the spiritual parents are being turned to
sons and daughters, and vice versa, just as it says in Malachi 4:5-
6. The power of these relationships insures succession and trans-

fer from generation to generation. They insure an increase in power and transference of authority. These are commonly called mentoring relationships—I also like to think of them as double-portion relationships.

SPIRITUAL FATHERS AND MOTHERS

When we survey history, we see that many church heroes had important mentors in their lives. Bruce Shelley points out that behind many of the Church's greatest leaders were powerful spiritual mothers and fathers. Here are a few examples:

- Behind Augustine, there was Monica, his biological mother, a devout Christian and tireless prayer warrior who prayed for her wandering prodigal until he was at last converted. Augustine later called Monica his mother both in the flesh and in the Lord.
- Behind Martin Luther was Johann Von Staupitz, a professor of Bible at the University in Wittenberg . . . When Luther became an Augustinian monk, Staupitz became his spiritual director and counselor. "If it had not been for Dr. Staupitz," Luther later said, "I should have sunk in hell." It was Staupitz who taught Luther about grace and directed him into the study of theology.
- Behind John Calvin was William Farel, who spurred Calvin on to courage and devotion. And when Calvin was dying, Farel left his own sickbed to come from afar to encourage Calvin.
- Behind John Wesley was Peter Boehler, of the Moravians, who seemed to possess what Wesley appeared to lack—a

personal, restful trust in God. It was by following Boehler's counsel that Wesley eventually found his heart "strangely warmed" at a midweek meeting on Aldersgate Street.

- Behind William Carey was Andrew Fuller, who had broken with the hyper-Calvinistic Baptist of his day and was appealing for people to be converted to Christ. Spurred on by Fuller's evangelistic zeal, Carey asked the logical question, "What about the people beyond our shores? Don't they, too, need the gospel?" The two men became soul-mates in missions, Carey in India, and Fuller, his mentor and supporter, cheering from the stands back home.[1]

Whether the mentor is cheering from the stands back home or walking side by side, God is restoring the "fellow worker" relationship of true spiritual parenting. It brings the exponential release that results in a double portion and greater works from one generation to another. If we are to be a generation that receives the accumulated prayers of previous generations, we must pursue these mentoring relationships. Many spiritual fathers and mothers are accepting their calling to parent and mentor, but many daughters and sons are running from the openness of transparency and true accountability.

Spiritual parents will keep us from duplicating the mistakes of the past and will propel us forward with increased purity and power. But it is important that the increased authority and power be sought after in the right ways and with proper motives. The relationship of Gehazi and Elisha shows potential pitfalls for today's spiritual sons and daughters. It also reveals the heart of a true spiritual father or mother through the example of Elisha. Though much still needs to be said about spiritual mothering and fathering, I will focus on sons and daughters and their function in these relationships.

A MODEL IN ELISHA

The prophet Elisha had some close and wealthy friends to whom he once ministered in Shunem (see 2 Kings 4:8-17). This woman and her husband made room for him at a time in his life when he was looking for shelter and food. Elisha, moved by the woman's generosity and hospitality, asked if there was anything that he could do for her. Her reply was basically, "No, I have everything I need. I have a nice house, and I can entertain if I want. I have a man who provides for me. I have food and clothes. I'm OK."

Elisha looked beyond the surface of her talk and said, "This time next year, you are going to have a son." To which she basically replied, "Don't toy with me. I'm going to bear a son? That is the greatest longing and desire of my heart." Elisha wasn't teasing her, and neither was God. The Lord rewarded her generosity, and she received a son as her prophet's reward.

A Prayer for Healing

Years went by, and her son was a growing 12-year-old. However, one day, that which she had hoped and longed for, her beautiful son, became sick and suddenly died. She sent out servants to look for her prophet friend, knowing that God was the only answer for her crisis. When Elisha found out about it, he sent his servant and spiritual son Gehazi to pray for the Shunammite woman's son (see 2 Kings 4:29-37).

In essence, Elisha said to Gehazi, "Take my staff (prayer rod), and place it on the child. Go and heal him in the name of the

Lord." Gehazi was given access to the Shunammite woman's home because she recognized Elisha's rod. But when Gehazi went to the child and placed it on his head, nothing happened. I'm sure Gehazi said all the right things, imitating everything he'd seen Elisha do. He may have even thought, *Hey, when Elisha received Elijah's mantle of authority, he said, "Where is the Lord, the God of Elijah?" I'll just use the same method and say, "Where is the Lord, the God of Elisha?"*

Whatever he did, it didn't work. Gehazi, with his lack of power and results, kindled more hopelessness, disappointment, despair and disillusionment in the friend of his spiritual father, Elisha. Later, Elisha showed up, persisted in prayer, stretched out over the dead boy, eye-to-eye and mouth-to-mouth, and the Lord healed and resurrected the boy. This question we must ask is, Why didn't the boy get healed when Gehazi came with Elisha's rod?

Gehazi's Mistake

This question plagued me for days. Then, one day I saw the heart of Gehazi as I read about the healing of Naaman the leper. Second Kings 5:19-25 says:

> He said to him, "Go in peace." So he departed from him some distance. But Gehazi, the servant of Elisha the man of God, thought, "Behold, my master [Elisha] has spared this Naaman the Aramean, by not receiving from his hands what he brought. As the LORD lives, I will run after him and take something from him."
>
> So Gehazi pursued Naaman. When Naaman saw one running after him, he came down from the chariot to meet him and said, "Is all well?" He said, "All is well. My master has sent me, saying, 'Behold, just now two young

men of the sons of the prophets have come to me from the hill country of Ephraim. Please give them a talent of silver and two changes of clothes.'"

Naaman said, "Be pleased to take two talents." And he urged him, and bound two talents of silver in two bags with two changes of clothes and gave them to two of his servants; and they carried them before him.

When he came to the hill, he took them from their hand and deposited them in the house, and he sent the men away, and they departed.

But he went in and stood before his master. And Elisha said to him, "Where have you been, Gehazi?" And he said, "Your servant went nowhere."

As mentioned, the context of this passage has to do with the healing of a leper named Naaman. Elisha refused to take an offering from Naaman. Gehazi, however, went to seek after the offering that had been turned down by Elisha. When he returned to his spiritual father, he even lied to him about having received it! God had already informed Elisha about it, however. (Gehazi wasn't too smart either. Lie to a prophet? Duh!) It was then that Gehazi not only lost the privilege of walking in intimate fellowship with his spiritual father but also the true condition of his heart, and his hidden motives were laid bare for all to see: He became a leper.

The Condition of the Heart

At last I understood why the little boy of the wealthy Shunammite woman had not been healed. God didn't allow Gehazi to be used in this healing because of the motives of his heart. Can God heal, or use us in other ways, in spite of us? Yes, He can and does. But in this story, the Lord is trying to take us deeper into His heart. God not only wants to use us *in spite of* us, but He also desires to use us *because of* us. He wants us to be vessels of honor, fit for every good work (2 Tim. 2:21). Too often we're fit for just a few good works.

God is looking to raise up sons and daughters with no hidden agendas, who have cleansed themselves of all defilement of the flesh and the spirit, perfecting holiness, growing in the fear of the Lord (2 Cor. 7:1). He wants to raise up holy, compassionate sons and daughters who desire His presence more than His provision, who carry His heart into hopeless situations and minister life without distorting His desires, image and reputation— sons and daughters who want the God of the rod more than they want the rod of God.

God, in His mercy, did not allow the wealthy woman to be taken advantage of by Gehazi in much the same way that he took advantage of Naaman's healing. God knew that the way to Naaman's and the Shunammite woman's hearts, because they were wealthy people, was to demonstrate His love by healing as a free gift. You cannot earn or buy a gift. The message God wanted to send was this: My love is priceless, and so are you.

Gehazi, however, had money, and perhaps other hidden motives, in his heart. He would have distorted God's image to this woman in much the same way that he later did with Naaman. God allowed Gehazi to carry Elisha's rod yet not heal in order to expose his bad heart. His lack of power should have led him back to the Power Source and to repentance before it was too late. This was Gehazi's merciful opportunity to deal with the issues in his heart before they were exposed and he was judged through leprosy.

Gehazi cared more about ministry and money than about representing the heart of God. Elisha, on the other hand, cared more about serving and relating with his own spiritual father,

Elijah, than about grabbing for his ministry. My friend Abbot "Red Cloud" Foster illustrates this powerfully. He wrote:

> Elisha served his prophet. Service, done in love and faith, is invested with spiritual power. "For even the Son of Man did not come to be served, but to serve, and to give His life as a ransom for many" (Mark 10:45). It is seed sown into the best soil: a spiritual father. Who is your prophet? Wash his hands. In other words, give rides, help with his house, anticipate his needs. Be his chief intercessor; mobilize prayer meetings. E. M. Bounds said, "The preacher must pray, and the preacher must be prayed for." Gehazi, Elisha's servant, had selfish motives: his own ministry and money. Elisha, though, when ministering to Elijah, got a passion to serve, wept for his father, and got the double portion.[2]

The first time I read this, it cut to the core of my being. I read this shortly after Dutch and I had made covenant together, and he had adopted me as one of his spiritual sons. One of the symbols of the covenant, given to me by Dutch, was a staff that had been given to him and symbolized authority. I remembered that Gehazi had received Elisha's prayer rod as well. I felt that the Lord was saying to me, "Will you be a son who serves and seeks true relationship, or will you be more concerned about ministry and money? Will you seek the God of the rod, or will you seek only the rod." Tears of conviction and godly sorrow led to a time of repentance. Hidden motives of my deceitful heart were laid bare. We don't always know our own hearts!

I feel that this lesson was not only for me but also for all of us. God is looking for sons and daughters who will serve, not so they can get what the mothers and fathers have: a name, a

ministry, an anointing and provision. He is asking a new generation of people, "Do you want to carry the rod like Gehazi or
carry it like Elisha?" God is looking for daughters and sons like
Elisha.

A Heart to Serve

Elisha was a son who emulated the life of the Son of God and
made himself of no reputation (see Phil. 2:6). Elisha saw equality with Elijah as nothing to be grasped and made himself a servant to his spiritual father. As a matter of fact, after being a
wealthy businessman, he emptied himself of his reputation; and
when Elijah called, he answered and served his spiritual father
(see 1 Kings 19:19-21). His reputation around town was as the
one who poured water over the hands of Elijah, not as the one
who got the double portion (see 2 Kings 3:11).

Elisha wept when his spiritual father was taken from him,
even as the mantle he prayed for was drifting in the wind toward
him! He gazed more at his ascending father than he did at the
falling mantle. And because he cared more about the relationship, he received Elijah's gifting and inheritance. Elisha received
the double portion because he cared more about relationship.
He knew that taking Elijah's mantle was equipping him for
Elijah's unfinished business: removing wicked Jezebel. His
acceptance of the mantle was more than just accepting authority; it was also accepting the responsibility of changing the
nation (see 1 Kings 19:16-17). Elisha was concerned with succession more than with originality.

Gehazi had other motives in mind. If he had received the
same promise as Elisha and was to be the successor to Elijah's
mantle, he would have been rejoicing rather than weeping as
Elijah went away. "Give me my mantle! Yes, it's finally all mine!"
would have been his cry. Sadly, little has changed. Where are the

sons and daughters who want relationships with their spiritual mothers and fathers more than they want their anointings and ministries?

A Son and His Rod

Gehazi was a son after inheritance. He reminds me of two other sons in Scripture who were after inheritance: the prodigal son and his elder brother. The prodigal son said, "Give me my inheritance" (see Luke 15:12). Basically, he was saying to his father, "I don't want you. I want your stuff."

"Give me my inheritance" is the cry of a rebellious heart. How much pain and how many church splits have happened in the Body of Christ because some young zealous son—who *went* out instead of being *sent* out—decided to take half of his inheritance—i.e., the congregation—with him? How many fathers in ministry today cannot retire because they have no pension and no other means of support and no sons they can trust? Their sons have moved on, and no one is taking care of them.

"I want your money" is the cry of the prodigal, while the other son who stayed at home, said, "Someday, this will all be mine." He too cares more about his inheritance than about his relationship with his father. He just conceals it better. When fallen sons are restored or new ones begin relationships, the heart of the elder brothers will be laid bare (see Luke 15:29). But hear the words of the father who modeled what is always the heart of a true mother or father: "All that I have is yours" (Luke 15:31, *NKJV*).

An Attitude Check

Elder brothers, are you rejoicing over your restored fallen brothers, or are you resentful over sharing with them again? Elder brothers, are you glad when the father brings in new sons, or are you making power plays, using politics and intimidation to protect your turf? Do you love your father, or do you love what he can provide? Are you more excited about access to your father or access to the inheritance?

The generosity of the mother's or father's heart always exposes this flaw. *More for me,* the elder brother thought. *Fool! I am glad he's gone.* But he failed to understand something about spiritual parents: A father or mother longs to gather fallen sons and daughters, and new ones as well.

A MODERN-DAY EXAMPLE

Dr. Edwin Louis Cole was the father of the Christian men's movement in America. When he was 59 years old, he left a successful church and started the Christian Men's Network. When he died at 80, his ministry was thriving in more than 210 nations! The key to his ministry was to build men and raise sons. Today many of his spiritual sons have some of the largest churches in the world.

When Dr. Cole died and his family made arrangements, I had a chance to spend time with his son, Paul Cole. Paul said that he realized that his father owned very little. He had no paintings or posters of himself; no monuments or busts to be passed down. Paul said, "Many men leave monuments as legacies, but my dad left spiritual sons as his legacy." Many of Dr. Cole's sons now have congregations as large as 25,000 members, and many are authors and powerful civic leaders. What many people don't know is that Dr. Cole had found many of his sons in broken relationships or experiencing setbacks before they were found in *Christianity Today* or *Charisma*. Dr. Cole visited these sons in storefront churches and prisons before they were on television. Dr. Cole's ministry to the Lord will go on because of what he instilled in Paul and in his spiritual sons. True spiritual leaders build up, raise up and stay with those relationships, regardless of success or failure. Fathering or mothering is their calling.

THE PASSING DOWN OF MANTLES

Father God is looking for spiritual daughters and sons who will be used to carry His rod of authority in the greatest revival in history. To see His power released through us, we must want God more than we want the rod. We must sanctify ourselves and become vessels of honor who are fit for every good work that He assigns to us in the days ahead. He is raising up double-portion sons and double-portion daughters whom He can trust with His power because they will not misrepresent His heart.

Gehazi hid his character flaws behind the rod of Elisha. He was able to enter the Shunammite woman's home because of Elisha's name and reputation, but he had no power from Heaven. We must not run the risk of name-dropping or of using other people's character to cover up our failings. If we do, we'll have a name that we are alive, but we will really be dead (see Rev. 3:1). We even run the risk of flippantly throwing around the rod of the name of Jesus, while our lack of power kindles more hopelessness and despair. We can try to use others' language, and even their strategies for success, to no avail. We must develop our own history with God. Mantles are passed down from one generation to the next, but they are not passed down the way we think they are.

I have three spiritual fathers. I serve and relate with them. One in particular (not Dutch) has a story that I want to share with you. This spiritual father had a natural father who had an enormous ministry. He was there when his father founded the ministry some 20 years ago. It had always been the dream of this spiritual father to take over his natural father's ministry. But when his father passed away, the board over the ministry voted for someone else to take the presidency instead of him. My spiritual father called me and asked me to pray during the time when he was to address the board. I was there, along with other friends and supporters of his, as well as friends and supporters of the new board-selected president. There was an awkward tension in the room as everyone wondered, *What is he going to say? How is he going to respond? If I were he, I would . . .*

After speaking for about 15 minutes, stating his rights and spending time talking about the Cross, my spiritual father summoned three people: his natural son, his son-in-law and the new president. His son carried a towel and his son-in-law carried a water pan. He then washed the feet of the board-selected president. Tears flooded many of our faces. It felt as if he were washing away jealousy, rejection, bitterness, competition and selfish agendas, cleansing his father's ministry as he washed the feet of the man who had displaced him.

The Lord spoke to me and said that many of us are just like Christ's disciples, hoping that our relationship with the Son will take us somewhere. The disciples were hoping that Jesus would be the Crown Prince who would overthrow the Roman government and that they would get to rule with Him: "We got a winner in this Jesus! It's not going to be those Pharisees; it's going to be us!" Judas wasn't the only one with a personal agenda.

The disciples felt disappointed, angry and disillusioned when Jesus forsook a palace and crown and led them to a wooden cross instead. But we shouldn't be so quick to look back and judge them. Many times, we won't know what's in our hearts until we are confronted with the crucible of testing that God has chosen for us.

When my spiritual father washed the feet of the new board-selected president, the Lord spoke to me that this man had chosen a cross instead of a crown. And in so doing, he had chosen a better resurrection, not only for himself, but also for those he fathers. When he picked up the towel, he picked up his father's mantle, and the true riches of a godly inheritance have fallen to him. He set himself up to receive his own visitation that will last for generations to come, because he chose the God of the rod, and not just the rod of his father's name. He sought the God of inheritance more than he sought the inheritance. But when he gave up the inheritance, spiritually he got it all—inheritance and mantle!

THE GOD OF THE ROD

How much more disillusionment should the world have to bear and how much more can Father God be grieved, as we use His rod for wrong motives—to build our own kingdoms instead of His? We scratch our heads as we try our Father's methods and formulas to no avail, because we are connected to the rod of God instead of being connected to the God of the rod. If we are not careful, our quest for power and money, just like Gehazi's, will take us to a place where we lose intimate fellowship with our heavenly Father. Then, like Gehazi, it won't be long before the leprous condition of our hearts is made manifest for the world to see.

God is exposing our lack of power and the wickedness of our hearts. How much longer will He allow us to misrepresent Him? We dare not test Him. We must sanctify ourselves and become double-portion sons and daughters. If we do not, we will pass on to the next generation the poison of our iniquity. The Bible says that all of Gehazi's household and descendants became leprous (see 2 Kings 5:26-27). Either we become daughters and sons who sanctify ourselves through the Cross, serve God and receive His double portion, or we will have our sin exposed and abort another move of God that could affect generations to come.

Will we be after the inheritance or the God of inheritance?

Notes
1. Bruce Shelley. Used by permission.
2. Abbot "Red Cloud" Foster, quoted in Jim W. Goll and Lou Engle, *Elijah's Revolution* (Shippensburg, PA: Treasure House Books, 2002), p. 183.

BREAKING GENERATIONAL CURSES

You shall not make for yourself an idol in the form of anything in heaven above or on the earth beneath or in the waters below. You shall not bow down to them or worship them; for I, the LORD your God, am a jealous God, punishing the children for the sin of the fathers to the third and fourth generation of those who hate me, but showing love to a thousand generations of those who love me and keep my commandments.

EXODUS 20:4-6, *NIV*

The following is a prayer plan that will help you partner with God to break generational curses and release generational blessing and inheritances. Honor God and accept His plan for the family you were born into while rejecting everything that has defiled it. Celebrate that which God has done and the liberty that He provided for you through His Son Jesus. When you follow the first part of Hebrews 12:1—laying aside the sin and weight that so easily besets you—you can experience the last part—running with endurance the race set before you. You can receive a pure baton from the former generation and run your race unhindered.

It takes courage to deal with these curses from the past, and we commend you. What you're about to do will affect not only you but also future generations in your family. Just as Josiah tore down the idols in his nation, once you deal with these issues and stand in the gap for your family, you can also stand in the gap for your nation. You may need to do some background study on your ancestry. Gain as much information as you can on your father's and your mother's side of your family tree. If that information doesn't exist, or if you're adopted and can't find any information on your ancestors, think about some of your own natural tendencies of temptation and struggles with sin. These could be areas in which your forebearers struggled and that are being passed down to your generation. Ask the Holy Spirit to bring to your mind the sins, weaknesses, breaches, curses, shortcomings and areas of vulnerability for which He wants you to stand in the gap. Identify and ask the Holy Spirit to bring to mind positive inherited attributes and godly attributes, and write these down as well.

Before you pray concerning past family sins or curses, you must make sure that you are free from personal sin. Ask the Holy Spirit to bring to your mind areas of unconfessed sin or unforgiveness. Once you have repented of personal sins and have released others whom you had not already forgiven, you will be ready to intercede. Here is a suggested pattern of prayer.

1. Deal with Personal Sins

Father God, I come to You in the name of Jesus, and thank You that You said that if I confess my sins, You are faithful and just to forgive me and cleanse me of all unrighteousness. You also say in Your Word in Psalm 24:3-4, "Who may ascend into the hill of the LORD? . . . He who has clean hands and a pure heart." So I come now, and I ask You to forgive me for the following sins [name them out loud and be open to the Holy Spirit to bring additional unconfessed sins to your mind]. *I plead the blood of Jesus over these areas of my life, and I thank You for forgiving me.*

I declare concerning every evil spirit that has had access into my life as a result of these sins, its power is broken and it must leave my presence now, in Jesus' name.

Dear Lord Jesus, You say that I am to forgive the same way that You have forgiven me. I choose to forgive and release the following people. I forgive _____ for_____ , and I release him/her to You. [Do this for each person on your list.] *Forgive me for my unforgiveness, and where there has been callousness, anger, bitterness, resentment and hurt, I release it all to You and ask You to heal me.*

Holy Spirit, I now ask that You fill me to overflowing with Your power and Your love. I ask that You cleanse me by the blood of Jesus from all unrighteousness. Thank You, Lord. You said that greater is He who is in me than He who is in the world. You have given us authority over all the power of the enemy.

I break the power of every tormenting, evil spirit and command you to leave my presence now, in Jesus' name.[1]

2. Deal with Generational Curses

Father, I thank You for my forefathers. I thank You for choosing me to be part of the family and family line You used to bring me into the world. I honor them, Lord, for You say in Your Word that if I honor them, it will be well with my soul. My parents and forefathers weren't perfect, for Your Word says that all have sinned and have fallen short of the glory of God. So right now, I forgive my forefathers for their sins and for opening the door to Satan in any way that has affected my life. I forgive my ancestors for [name any sins you are aware of]. *Also, I accept my responsibility for participating in these sins, and for keeping the door open and affecting future generations. Forgive me for my participation as well.*

I stand in the gap for my family, and I ask You to forgive us for opening the door to destruction in our family and turning away from You. Forgive me for how I've hurt other people with my sins. Forgive me and my family for pacts we've made with the enemy, known and unknown, through witchcraft, the occult, paganism and all false religions—even idolatry of money and possessions. We thank You, Lord Jesus, that You became a curse for us, because in Galatians 3:13, Your Word says, "Cursed is everyone who hangs on a tree." You have made provision for the breaking of all curses.

I appropriate the power of the Cross in my family now. I ask that You cleanse us, Lord, with Your blood. I now take the authority that You have given us and break the power of every generational curse that has come on my family. I break the power of all generational sin going back three and four generations, and I break the power of every curse in our family. I cancel the power and effect on my children as well.

I command every spirit that has had access into my life as a result my forefathers' sins to leave my presence now, in Jesus name.[2]

3. Call Forth Generational Blessings and Callings

I declare that sin patterns and curses that have affected me and my children are now broken. I now claim deliverance and shut the door to these sins and curses, and I ask You to place Your cross, Jesus, over these areas. I now open the door to generational blessings and call forth the positive and godly attributes of [name any gifts and righteous attributes you know of in your family history]. *I call forth every righteous root from my descendants, in Jesus' name. I now claim generational blessings for myself and my children. I claim the spiritual inheritance in Christ that is to be released to me through my forefathers. I lay hold of the mantle of godliness that they had and lay hold of God's purpose and destiny for my family. I come into agreement with the righteous prayers of my forefathers, and all prayers that*

are to be answered through us. I receive those callings and assign-
ments, Lord. I bind myself to You, Jesus, for Your yoke is easy,
and Your burden is light. Release the latter-rain glory in my fam-
ily and in this nation.

I ask for generational blessings to go forth to a thousand gen-
erations or until You return, Jesus. I ask that You would use my
life to bring blessing, fruitfulness and prosperity to the next gen-
eration. I release to them a double portion of the mantle that You
have given me. I also ask for spiritual sons and daughters of dif-
ferent ages and races so that every tribe and tongue, and genera-
tions yet to be created, may praise You, Lord. Thank You for
freedom and for the freedom of the next generation.[3]

Notes

1. See 1 John 1:9; Psalm 24:3-4; Matthew 18:18; 1 John 4:4; Luke 10:19;
   Matthew 18:18.
2. See Deuteronomy 5:16; Romans 3:23; Deuteronomy 5:9; Psalm 79:8;
   Ecclesiastes 9:18; Deuteronomy 18:10; Galatians 3:13; Deuteronomy 23:2.
3. See Job 22:28; Matthew 16:19; Isaiah 22:22; Isaiah 61:7; Jeremiah 29:7;
   Hosea 11:4; Matthew 11:30; Proverbs 16:15; Zechariah 10:1; Deuteronomy
   5:10; 2 Kings 2:9; Isaiah 61:7; Psalm 78:6.

For information about other resources or to contact
Dutch Sheets and Will Ford, call or write:

DUTCH SHEETS MINISTRIES
3945 N. Academy Blvd.
Colorado Springs, CO 80917
Phone: (719) 548-8226
FAX: (719) 548-8793

Contact them by e-mail at
ministryinfo@dutchsheets.org for Dutch Sheets and
w.ford@verizon.net for Will Ford.

You can also visit their websites:

www.dutchsheets.org

www.willfordministries.org

More Books on Prayer from Dutch Sheets

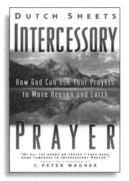
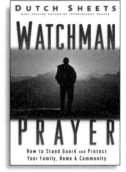
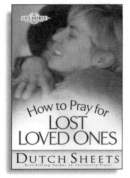
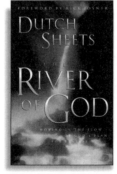
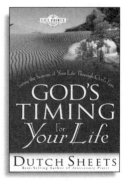